UNHEARD VOICES

UNHEARD VOICES

The Effects of Silence on Lesbian and Gay Educators

RONNI L. SANLO

BERGIN & GARVEY
Westport, Connecticut • London

Library of Congress Cataloging-in-Publication Data

Sanlo, Ronni L., 1947–
    Unheard voices : the effects of silence on lesbian and gay
educators / Ronni L. Sanlo.
        p.   cm.
    Includes bibliographical references (p.   ) and index.
    ISBN 0–89789–640–8 (alk. paper)
    1. Lesbian teachers—Florida Interviews.   2. Gay teachers—Florida
Interviews.   I. Title.
    LB2844.1.G39S36   1999
    371.1′008′664—dc21   99–22082

British Library Cataloguing in Publication Data is available.

Library of Congress Catalog Card Number: 99–22082
ISBN: 0–89789–640–8

First published in 1999

Bergin & Garvey, 88 Post Road West, Westport, CT 06881
An imprint of Greenwood Publishing Group, Inc.
www.greenwood.com

Printed in the United States of America

The paper used in this book complies with the
Permanent Paper Standard issued by the National
Information Standards Organization (Z39.48–1984).

10 9 8 7 6 5 4 3 2 1

To my beloved granddaughters

Elizabeth and Calista

Contents

Illustrations   ix

Acknowledgments   xi

Introduction   xv
    Purpose   xvii
    Definition of Terminology   xviii
    Overview   xx

1   In the Beginning There Was Public Education   1

2   Lesbian and Gay Educators: Documenting Their Existence   5
    A Brief History of Lesbian and Gay People   6
    Laws Affecting Teachers   10
    Lesbian and Gay Teachers in Florida and Northeast Florida   12

3   Methodology: The Participants and the Process   21
    The Use of Qualitative Methodology to Interview Lesbian
      and Gay Educators   21
    How Northeast Florida Teachers Were Selected for the Study   23
    The Participants   25
    Ethical Concerns   27
    Data Analysis   28
    Theoretical Framework for Analysis   31
    The Questions: A Plan for Data Collection   32

4 The Silence Breaks: Voices of the Teachers   35
        Barry   36
        Barbra   43
        Len   48
        Elisa   59
        Sherry   68

5 Making Meaning of Their Words   79
        Introduction of the Participants   82
        Their Lives and Their Experiences   84

6 Creating Change: Envisioning the Future   121
        The Possibilities   124
        Recommendations for Further Research   128
        Conclusion   129

Resources and Recommended Reading   131

References   133

Index   141

Illustrations

Table 1   Key Words and Phrases Used in Coding   29

Figure 1   Interpretive Model: How Lesbian and Gay   80
                  Teachers View Their World

Acknowledgments

This work was originally submitted and accepted as my doctoral dissertation by the University of North Florida (UNF) College of Education in Jacksonville, Florida. I extend my thanks to the Greenwood Publishing Group and especially to Jane Garry for providing the opportunity to make it available in this format, and to Nicole Cournoyer, production editor at Greenwood, who provided patient and detailed editing assistance throughout the final preparations. I offer deep and sincere thanks and appreciation to my dissertation committee chair, Dr. Elinor Scheirer, for her expertise, skill, and extreme patience. She spent a tremendous amount of time and energy with me and my dissertation manuscript. Although she chairs numerous dissertation committees, Dr. Scheirer told me that the only other dissertation to which she devoted so much time was her own. Without her guidance and belief in justice, this work might look quite different. In addition, I owe a debt of gratitude to the other members of my dissertation committee, not only for their educational support but also for their advocating that I write this book: Dr. Tom Serwatka, whose gentle nagging and numerous brunches were the perfect accompaniments to Dr. Scheirer's energy; Dr. G. Pritchy Smith, who introduced me to multiculturalism; Dr. Ken Wilburn, who brought the concept of "centering" into my program; and Dr. Miner Chamblin, the "Dr. Ruth" of UNF. They each offered their own special brand of support throughout my doctoral work. Finally, I extend my thanks to Dr. Kathe Kasten, dean of the University of North Florida College of Education and Human Services, who offered genuine support from my first interview for the doctoral program through the writing of my dissertation.

I am deeply appreciative of the interactive collegial support of the members of the UNF Doctoral Cohort Two. We all grew from the camaraderie and sustenance we gave one another as we learned together. I especially wish to thank Cohort colleagues Dr. Jeanne Borstein for her wordsmithing skills and hospitality and Dr. Jim Langen for his conversations with me about theoretical screens. Both helped me make sense of this work when it seemed as if it were little more than nonsensical reams of paper. Ken Blochowski, my friend and colleague at the University of Michigan, provided the graphics for the theoretical screen as I sought to explain to him exactly what I was trying to convey.

My dear friends Frieda and Len Saraga opened their home to me as I commuted between the University of North Florida, where I was a doctoral student, and the University of Michigan, where I was employed. Their enduring love and hospitality made each trip gentle and pleasant. Years ago, Frieda saw in me what I could not see in myself. With her love and occasional gentle prodding, I was able to find my way into the future. I remain deeply grateful for her persistent love and friendship.

In 1989, when I was a first-year masters level student at UNF, Dr. Travis Carter suggested (in writing, thank you, Dr. Carter) that I consider doing doctoral work. His words of encouragement inadvertently brought back the nightmare of that horrid undergraduate academic counselor at the University of Florida —whose name I promptly forgot and now wish I had not—who in 1965 told me I was not college material.

I extend deep thanks to my former supervisor and friend, Royster Harper, dean of students at the University of Michigan, for her encouragement and enthusiasm as I approached completion of my dissertation. Kathy Lindblad spent much time reading, opining, offering editorial assistance, and preparing gallons of coffee for the initial dissertation. Andrea Constancio was an immeasurable source of assistance, both with my dissertation process and with the rewriting of the dissertation into book format. She was a second set of hands for me at Michigan and is a faithful friend at UCLA.

My parents, Sanford and Lois Lebman, and my siblings—Sherry and Barry Horwitz, Len and Carole Engstrom-Lebman, and Barbra and Hal Miner—were my greatest cheerleaders as I completed this work. Since my graduation from UNF in 1996, my parents have become active members of Parents and Friends of Lesbians and Gays (PFLAG) in Ventura, California. I am extremely proud of them.

Bill Watson has been the editor of *The Weekly News* (TWN), Florida's lesbian and gay newspaper, for more than 20 years. He was very gracious in opening the doors and archives of TWN to me. He located volumes of important old papers, then left me to my own devices. I was searching for specific information for this work, but found so much more. My own history as a lesbian, a Floridian, and as a budding leader 20 years ago, danced on the yellowing, brittle pages of old TWN issues. Thank you, Bill, for keeping our history alive.

My children were taken from me when they were 2 and 5 because of my sexual orientation. Twenty years later, an acknowledgement of thanks to my daughter, Berit—who presented me with 2 granddaughters as this book was being written—is not enough. She had the courage and took the time to reconnect with me after years of separation. Our relationship is growing, along with the number of our family members, thanks to her and her husband, Mark. My son, Erik, also courageously contacted me and returned to my life as this book was being completed. For my beautiful children and grandchildren, I am deeply, deeply thankful.

My partner, Rose Maly, is my rock and my heart. She provides the stability—and the laughter—in my life. She teaches me daily about love, about balance, and about living each day is if it was our last. Her patience, strength, and powerful love are irreplaceable.

I offer deep and tender thanks to my lesbian, gay, bisexual, and transgender (LGBT) students and staff at the UCLA LGBT Campus Resource Center who remind me daily with their passion, courage, and hope exactly why this work is necessary. They will carry the work forward in making this world a kinder, gentler place.

Finally, in awe and with great respect, I extend my deepest gratitude to the lesbian and gay teachers of northeast Florida who participated in this study. Despite their fears, they opened their hearts and entrusted me with their stories. Their journeys and their words will join others in paving the way for safety and freedom for young people coming up and coming out behind us.

Introduction

Sixteen lesbian and gay public school teachers took the risk of their lives, opened their hearts, and filled the pages of this book with their untold stories. To be a lesbian or gay person is not easy; it is fraught with society's challenges about who we think people must be. Lesbian and gay people who are teachers in the public school system must live with the added stress of identity management and fear of discovery just to remain employed.

The teachers whose lives are documented here are from the northeast Florida area which was selected for study for several reasons. First, there is no documentation regarding the experiences of lesbian and gay teachers in this part of the country. Second, there is a large and thriving lesbian and gay community in northeast Florida, despite the preponderance of typically homophobic southern influence. Finally, although the northeast Florida area is part of the Deep South, this region likely shares characteristics in common with many other regions of the United States. Therefore, all educators and people concerned about equity and fairness in the teaching profession throughout the United States may find this study relevant.

Lesbian, gay, bisexual, and transgender (LGBT) teachers often perceive themselves to be invisible and isolated (Harbeck, 1992a, 1997; Khayatt, 1992; Krysiak, 1987; McNaron, 1997). In geographical areas where homosexuality, bisexuality, or gender identity are not discussed in the public schools, invisibility is heightened. Outside such areas as Los Angeles, New York City, and San Francisco, sketchy documentation, little acknowledgment, and few support systems exist for LGBT teachers in the context of the public schools.

Society's past and current expectations of teachers do not consider the concept that they may be gay or lesbian (Sciullo, 1984). Sciullo (1984) noted that it is nearly impossible for a teacher to continue in the classroom once she or he is labeled, voluntarily or not, accurately or not, as gay or lesbian. Harbeck (1992a) and more recently Kissen (1996a) indicate that this condition has not changed. As recently as 1997 in Utah (First Amendment Center, 1997) and 1998 in California (Glionna, 1998), teachers were publicly harassed or forced to resign their teaching positions when their sexual orientation became known.

Harbeck (1992a, 121) stated that "although society has been confronted with the issue of the homosexual schoolteacher since Socrates educated the youth of Greece, little is known about this often invisible but highly emotionally arousing educational concern." Griffin (1992a, 167) agreed that due to invisibility and to "the stigma attached to research on homosexuality in education, little is known about gay and lesbian [or bisexual or transgender] educators." Based on the literature, one can assume that LGBT teachers are likely to be invisible as a result of their silence due to local communities' implicit or implied demands. Their experience of being silent and invisible needs to be more fully understood so that all members of the community may become aware of its inherent diversity and complexity. Such awareness could then lead to efforts designed to maximize the contributions of all people for the common good.

This study, therefore, was designed to investigate what it means for lesbian and gay teachers to work in public schools where the larger community appears to support the silence about their experiences. Because an example of such a community setting is the northeast Florida region, this study specifically explored what it means to be a lesbian or gay teacher in the public school setting there. It is important to note that no teacher who was interviewed identified as bisexual or transgender, nor did they know any student or colleague who identified as such. Because no bisexual or transgender persons were included in this work, there is little mention of them. However, it is my belief that the experience of bisexual and transgender people, especially around issues of silence, invisibility and discrimination, is likely very similar to those of lesbian and gay people.

Harbeck (1992a) argued that the focus of research must address the experiences of lesbian and gay educators because so little is known about their lives. She listed questions that should be considered when researching this population of teachers. For example, she wondered about the degree to which lesbian and gay teachers feel free to reveal their sexual orientation and to whom they might reveal it. Of interest, as well, are the tensions created in the professional lives of lesbian and gay teachers as a result of their sexual orientation; how their sexual orientation has affected relationships with students, especially lesbian and gay students; and how their sexual orientation has affected peer and colleague relationships. The absence of information about these issues as delineated by Harbeck was a primary motivation for this research.

The dearth of literature about their lives leads to the conclusion that more needs to be known about the professional work experiences of lesbian and gay teachers. Although Harbeck (1992a, 1997), Jennings (1994), Khayatt (1992), Kissen (1996a), and Olson (1987) have explored the lives of lesbian and gay teachers, there are few articles, theses, and dissertations that focus on the experiences of these educators in the classroom.

PURPOSE

The purpose of this research was to explore the experiences of and provide a vehicle for the voices of lesbian and gay public school teachers in one area of the country. It was designed to discover answers to the following questions: Why do lesbians and gay men become teachers? What social or professional difficulties do they encounter? Why do they remain in the teaching profession? This book documents the experiences of 16 lesbian and gay educators in an attempt to learn how their sexual orientation affected their experiences within the school setting.

A benefit that may result from this research is that lesbian and gay educators themselves may learn from their colleagues who participated in this study. Although they may not acknowledge their sexual orientation openly in the public school system, they may see the similarities in their own lives through the documented experiences revealed by the gay and lesbian educators in northeast Florida.

Tierney et al. (1992, 11) argued that lesbian and gay educators need to speak up; otherwise, their concerns "will likely go unnoticed amid the common assumptions that all people are heterosexual, or that those who are not do not deserve the same opportunities and protections extended to others." When Khayatt (1992) interviewed lesbian teachers in Ontario, Canada, she saw that by their silence they contributed to their own isolation.

This book reveals the ways some lesbian and gay teachers experience the educational process, how they view themselves, and how they interact with their students, colleagues, and supervisors, thereby adding to a growing body of literature about lesbian and gay people. It also supplies a building block for the inclusion of gay and lesbian teachers in the public school system. Finally, it provides a rationale for teachers and administrators to support and include lesbian and gay issues, people, and events in the usual curricular content. Such inclusion is necessary for numerous reasons: to remove the secrecy about and the isolation of lesbian and gay teachers in public schools; to ensure equal opportunity in education regardless of sexual orientation; to reduce discrimination and harassment based on sexual orientation in the educational setting; and to teach a full range of diversity which is inclusive of all students, faculty, and staff.

DEFINITION OF TERMINOLOGY

Confusion may arise regarding the definitions of significant terms frequently used to describe lesbian and gay people. Since some terminology used in this book might be foreign to the reader, words necessary for the understanding of experiences of gay and lesbian people are defined here. *Faggot, dyke, pervert, sissy, fag, lezzie, girlfriend,* and *queer* are derogatory nouns that have been used to defame and demoralize lesbian and gay people. However, these terms are affectionately used within the gay community as inclusive language without negative connotations. Some of these terms—especially *queer* and *dyke*—have been embraced by the gay and lesbian community as terms of positive description and empowerment.

Heterosexual, homosexual, and *bisexual* are terms that describe sexual orientation and attraction. The words *heterosexual* and *homosexual* were first used in the 1860s in Germany (Khayatt, 1992). Khayatt (1992, 62) explained that "*heterosexuality* became a term of convenience to distinguish those who practiced normative sexuality from those who were, in the late nineteenth century, being discovered as abnormal or perverted according to definitions developed in that era."

In this work, a person identified as *homosexual* is sexually attracted to persons of the same sex. A person who is *heterosexual* is sexually attracted to persons of the other sex. A non-pejorative slang term for a heterosexual person is *straight*. A *bisexual* person is sexually attracted to persons of either sex though not necessarily simultaneously. According to the National Education Association (1991, 20), homosexuality, like heterosexuality, is "normal, has no known cause, and is not an illness."

The terms *lesbian* and *gay* are used in this book to describe women and men whose sexual orientations are homosexual and whose emotional, sexual, and affectional feelings are directed toward individuals of the same sex (Harbeck, 1992a; Khayatt, 1992). *Coming out of the closet* or *coming out* means to reveal one's sexual orientation, generally first to self and then to others. The process of coming out continues throughout one's life (Berzon, 1992; Harbeck, 1992a; Pope, 1995; Sears, 1991; Tierney, et al., 1992).

Homophobia is defined as a fear, hatred, or intolerance of, or discomfort with, people who are homosexual (Blumenfeld, 1992; Harbeck, 1992a; National Education Association, 1991; Schreier, 1995; Sears, 1992a). Friedman and Downey (1994) offered an interesting description of people who are homophobic: They are generally religious, conservative, and authoritarian; their negative views of homosexuality are perceived as normal; and they are not aware of having personal contact with people who are lesbian or gay.

Blumenfeld (1992) and Harbeck (1992a) noted that it is nearly impossible for lesbian and gay teachers to speak up and speak out in the public schools. *Internalized homophobia*—hatred of one's own homosexuality and intense fear of exposure—paralyzes lesbian and gay teachers; they are unable to come to their own defense or to the defense of lesbian and gay adolescents in their classrooms. Such paralysis prevents these teachers from aiding a student who is experiencing harassment, from noting famous or heroic lesbian and gay people within the context of lessons being taught, and from being a positive role model for all adolescents.

Blumenfeld (1992) described *institutional homophobia* as that which allows lesbian and gay people to experience systematic discrimination through laws, codes, or policies. Such homophobia works to legitimize oppression within groups of people. Tierney et al. (1992) documented that a homophobic environment in the educational setting forces gay and lesbian teachers to measure and process everything in their lives. Homophobia affects teachers' interactions with students and colleagues, as well as with the material they teach and the manner in which they teach it. Tierney and his colleagues added that homophobia means that educators live with the fear "that disclosure of their sexual orientation will destroy their professional careers, deprive them of the rewards of their scholarship, and/or cause them to be fired or denied tenure" (1992, 49).

Heterosexism is defined as the assumption that only heterosexuality is good and proper and that all people who are heterosexual have the right to dominate those who are not heterosexual (Blumenfeld, 1992; National Education Association, 1991; Schreier, 1995). Additional terms frequently used by the lesbian and gay community appear in this book. An *ally* is an advocate, one who stands up for and supports lesbian and gay people.

Allies reach across differences to help achieve mutual goals (Zuckerman & Simons, 1994). *Domestic partners* or *partners* are people who "live together in an intimate long-term relationship of indefinite duration, with an exclusive mutual commitment similar to that of marriage, in which the partners share the necessities of life and agree to be financially responsible for each others' [*sic*] well-being" (Fried et al., 1994, 1). Some municipalities offer a registration process similar to a marriage license registration as an acknowledgment of domestic partnership.

The term *community* is used throughout this book in reference to the lesbian and gay community, the educational community, and the greater northeast Florida community. Kindred, Bagin, and Gallagher (1990, 22) defined *community* as a group of people "who are organized around special interests." They added that some community groups are in conflict, while others are "highly cooperative with those who hold similar interests." Some community groups are more organized and politicized, while others exist informally based on common beliefs.

OVERVIEW

Chapter 1 provides a brief foundational overview of public education in the United States. Relevant literature is reviewed in chapter 2, which offers a snapshot history of lesbian and gay people, primarily as that history relates to culture and community. It also reviews legal issues that are pertinent to lesbian and gay people in general and lesbian and gay educators in particular. Finally, it combines the historical and legal perspectives to offer background on the experiences of lesbian and gay educators in Florida and northeast Florida.

Chapter 3 discusses the methodology used to collect the data, as well as the construction of the theoretical screen through which data was sifted for analysis and interpretation. The nature and structure of the initial research question (what is it like to be a lesbian or gay teacher in northeast Florida) mandated the use of a qualitative research approach, the selection of which reflected the intention to detail the complexity of people's lives. The voices of some of the participants through their transcripts are presented in chapter 4 while chapter 5 describes the interpretive model developed from the analysis of the data. Each section in chapter 5 presents a particular theme or concept relevant to the participants. At the end of each section, a summary describes the data that emerged from the stories and experiences shared by this small self-selected population of lesbian and gay public school teachers in northeast Florida.

Chapter 6 summarizes the analysis and interpretation of the data collected in this work. It also offers specific recommendations for the school districts in northeast Florida that could easily be translated for appropriate use in any school district in the country. Such recommendations were found throughout the literature, as well as in the data collected during interviews with the participants. This chapter also details areas for further research efforts.

This work could have emerged from any school district in the country, but Florida in general and northeast Florida specifically were chosen because they were my home. Although I now live in Los Angeles and work at UCLA, I am a product of the Florida public school system, from grade school through a bachelor's degree from the University of Florida to an M.Ed. and an Ed.D. in educational leadership from the University of North Florida. My two children—of whom I lost custody when they were very young because of my sexual orientation—made similar educational journeys, and soon my granddaughters will enter that same system. When I was an adolescent just beginning to understand that I was not heterosexual, I felt incredibly unsafe and intensely alone in the Florida school system. There has been little change there in the 40-some years since I discovered my sexual orientation. The silence, the lack of role models, the invisibility in the curriculum, and the unrelenting intolerance of Florida laws have not changed much although glimmers of hope periodically shine through.

The educators in this study provided such glimmers by offering their stories. Despite their immeasurable fear of discovery, they chose to share their experiences so that change could begin, if not for them then for their students and for future generations of educators. This work is transferable to other locations; sadly, the results would likely be similar in other communities in Florida, in the South, and throughout the country. It is my hope—and the hope of these educators—that this work and the growing body of literature addressing sexual orientation and gender identity issues in public schools will have a positive impact. Hopefully, our future generations—my granddaughters' perhaps—will be served by courageous educational leaders, and schools will finally be transformed from places of terror to places of safety and welcome.

UNHEARD VOICES

Chapter 1

In the Beginning There Was Public Education

The image of the public school teacher has changed since colonial times. The gangling, stick-figured Ichabod Crane riding his bony horse through one's mind's eye was the stereotypical teacher of the early period of U.S. history. Coinciding in time with the development of the common school and the government's concern with public education during the first half of the nineteenth century, Ichabod's male colleagues either headed west for adventure or stayed in the populated urban areas to pursue economic opportunities outside the field of education. By the mid-1800s it was clear that although teaching did not promise great financial reward, teachers were needed. With great exuberance but little education themselves, women responded in large numbers to the call to join the profession (Altenbaugh, 1992; Donovan, 1938; Urban, 1982). As a result, teaching became institutionalized as a continuing employment opportunity for women—a second-class population—while providing only temporary employment for men (Lortie, 1975).

In general, the teaching profession in this country has been held in fairly high esteem (Lortie, 1975). However, both Donovan (1938) and Lortie (1975) noted that teachers were not individually valued as members of communities; others often circumscribed their lives and social activities. Society's expectations of teachers as described historically by Donovan (1938), Lortie (1975), and Sciullo (1984) did not include the concepts of individuality, private lives, or respect for difference. A teacher's existence was often one in which his or her every move and mood were scrutinized by the community in which he or she lived

(Donovan, 1938). In 1938, Donovan warned that those teachers who were perceived as different from their peers could be forced to leave the teaching profession. This warning may well have set the tone for the isolation of lesbian and gay teachers from their heterosexual colleagues today.

Altenbaugh (1992) described a more current, though similar, perception of the ambivalent relationship U.S. teachers have with the communities in which they live. Citizens in most communities still tend to scrutinize what is taught in the classroom, a process which is exemplified by the current debates nationally over the role of religion, the inclusion of sexuality education, and library book censorship. Such citizens also tend to monitor teachers' public, private, and social behaviors outside the classroom.

Historically, teachers in the United States have been considered by communities as role models for students (Donovan, 1938; Jersild, 1955; Harbeck, 1992a). Adherence to higher moral standards than those required of average citizens has often been a requirement for teachers who wished to remain in the classroom. Moral lives have been defined by the values of particular locales. Such expectations of exemplary behavior have served to isolate teachers from the communities in which they live. However, as teachers have become active members in their communities and have interacted fully with other community members, opportunities for others to obtain personal knowledge about teachers have increased. At the same time, lesbian and gay teachers have had cause to seek isolation because of their differences from their peers.

Teachers appear to live at the whim of their communities, each of which seems to represent a variety of standards. U.S. courts have often been asked to intervene in an effort to create definitions of such standards. According to Newman (1990), judicial groups have affirmed or rejected a teacher's right to continue teaching based on the circumstances of each case. Both Newman (1990) and Altenbaugh (1992) noted cases that violated community standards and provided causes for termination from the local public school systems. Historically, such examples have included unmarried teachers who became pregnant, unmarried teachers who lived with someone of the other sex, married women who hid their marriages to remain employed, and, more recently, lesbian and gay teachers whose sexual orientation became known.

Teachers who are aware that they do not match society's standards may internalize these perceptions. It is also likely that such reactions lead to silence about who they are. This response pattern could then negatively affect their view of themselves, their classroom performance, and their ability to interact fully with students, colleagues, and administrators.

Chapter 2

Lesbian and Gay Educators: Documenting Their Existence

The review of literature for this work began with a search for validation and documentation that lesbian and gay educators in fact exist, as well as for what already had been discovered about them. Next, the review examined legal perspectives, since cases related to sexual orientation and education have been addressed in courts across the United States in recent years. The legal review reflects the scrutiny under which "teachers' behavior, habits, routines, and practices outside of their classroom" (Schneider-Vogel, 1986, 285) have fallen over the years. It also substantiates that lesbian and gay teachers who are open about their sexual orientation face the possibility of being terminated from their teaching positions (Harbeck, 1992b; Kissen, 1996a; Schneider-Vogel, 1986).

Available literature that specifically describes the lives and experiences of lesbian and gay educators is limited. Barale (1989) looked at the experiences of teachers from a feminist perspective, focusing only on lesbians. Olson (1987), Griffin (1992a, 1992b), and Khayatt (1992) researched ways in which teachers managed information regarding their sexual identity. Juul and Repa (1993) and Croteau and Lark (1995) studied the topic of job satisfaction among lesbian and gay people in education, particularly as it related to one's being out of the closet. Mayer (1993) conducted a study comparing the self-acceptance of gay and lesbian teachers to that of heterosexual teachers. Jennings (1994) edited a volume of personal stories of lesbian and gay teachers. Griffin (1992b, 25) noted that many of the participants in these studies resented "the injustice of having to maintain a double life, lie to colleagues and students, and endure the anti-gay attitudes and actions they encounter at school."

The literature review for this work focused on lesbian and gay teachers in general, and on lesbian and gay teachers in Florida and northeast Florida in particular. Although research is beginning to appear regarding lesbian and gay teachers in general, documentation of the specific experiences of gay and lesbian teachers in particular geographic areas of the country remains scant. Just as lesbian and gay teachers in northeast Florida are silent about their sexual orientation, so is the literature on their existence and their experiences.

A BRIEF HISTORY OF LESBIAN AND GAY PEOPLE

Although gay and lesbian people are woven into the fabric of humankind throughout history, a few significant events are briefly introduced here in order to provide and clarify informational background. Boswell (1980) described the early existence of lesbian and gay people and Christianity's response to them up to the fourteenth century. His extensive research of biblical passages and multiple translations found nothing that contained the equivalent of the word or words to mean homosexuality. Both Boswell (1980) and Duberman (1991) explained that the principal texts of the Bible that are generally used today to condemn homosexuality were actually referring quite specifically to temple prostitution, uncleanliness, and masturbation.

Boswell (1980) pointed out that until the eleventh century, gay and lesbian people were equal members of medieval societies. Duberman (1991) found, however, that between the mid–twelfth to mid–fourteenth centuries, attitudes toward homosexuality underwent a dramatic change.

The personal preference of a prosperous minority, satirized and celebrated in popular verse, [became] a dangerous, antisocial, and severely sinful aberration. What had been morally and legally acceptable in 1100 A.D. was by 1300 A.D. regarded as an activity subject to the death penalty—often for a single proven act. Why this dramatic transformation in public opinion? We don't know. (Duberman, 1991, 378)

In 1566, in the Spanish colony of St. Augustine, Florida, in the New World of America, a gay man was sentenced to death because of his sexual orientation. Katz (1976) documented that this event in Florida was the first recorded execution related to homosexuality in the United States.

Beginning in 1864 in Germany with the studies of Karl Ulrichs, there was "a proliferation of literary and scientific works" (Lauritsen & Thorstad, 1974, 9) that addressed homosexuality. In 1897, German educator Magnus Hirschfeld founded the Scientific Humanitarian Committee, the first gay liberation organization to insure that the oppression of lesbians and gay men be recognized as a significant form of discrimination and be eliminated. He also founded the World League for Sexual Reform in 1921 in Berlin. On May 6, 1933, Hirschfield was killed by the Nazis, and more than 10,000 volumes from his Institute for Sexual Science were destroyed, as the Nazis attempted to cleanse the libraries "of books of 'un-German' spirit" (Lauritsen & Thorstad, 1974, 40). This action initiated the destruction of books and literature throughout Germany.

Heger (1980), Lauritsen and Thorstad (1974), and Plant (1986) noted that prior to Hitler's rise to power, homosexuality was not condemned in Germany, although it was not legally condoned. Paragraph 175 of the German Penal Code, written in 1871, outlawing homosexuality, was generally ignored by law enforcement agencies. The modern gay rights movement began in Germany in 1869, where it paved the way for quiet acceptance of lesbians and gay men. However, when the Nazi regime rose to its full force, Paragraph 175 was invoked and homosexuality was once again a crime for which one could be prosecuted. Gay men were taken to the concentration camps and identified by pink triangles that were intended as signs of effeminacy and weakness. Lesbians were forced to wear the black or red triangle that classified them as political prisoners (Fischer, 1994). They were sent to "Spring of Life" homes where Nazi soldiers impregnated them against their will to replenish the Aryan nation. Heger (1980) and Plant (1986) explained that when the camps were liberated by Allied forces, lesbian and gay people, unlike the other prisons of war, were not released from the camps but were sent to German prisons as criminals in violation of German Penal Code Paragraph 175. Homosexuality remained illegal, and gay and lesbian people remained imprisoned for more than 20 years until 1968 when Paragraph 175 was finally abolished.

Lauritsen and Thorstad (1974) noted that during the late 1800s, there was little or no organized activity to obtain equal rights for gays and lesbians in the United States. Weiss and Schiller (1988, 12) referred to the early part of the twentieth century as "the twilight world" when homosexuality was never discussed, but gay life proliferated in party-type fashion in the larger cities. They noted that politically the 1950s was a depressing, repressive period of time for lesbians and gay men, particularly in the face of McCarthyism and investigations by the U.S. House UnAmerican Activities Committee. Nonetheless, during that decade the Mattachine Society and Daughters of Bilitis, the first national organizations for gay men and lesbians respectively, were founded. The goals of these organizations were to provide support for gay men and lesbians, as well as to provide education to the general public about gay and lesbian people.

Weiss and Schiller (1988) documented the tumultuousness of the 1960s. Homosexuality was a topic of conversation by medical experts and religious leaders. It was also occasionally discussed in popular national magazines. This attention to the topic was in contrast to the silence or veiled innuendoes that had previously appeared in the media. Writer Barbara Gittings acknowledged that "one of the major successes of the gay movement of the 1960s was our breakthrough into mainstream publicity" (Weiss & Schiller, 1988, 56). Then Stonewall happened.

On the night of June 27, 1969, hundreds of gay men poured out of the Stonewall Inn in New York City's Greenwich Village, hurling bricks and bottles at police. No longer willing to put up with police harassment that included the routine arrest of patrons of this and many other gay bars, gay people fought back and sparked three days of rioting in the streets. This explosion of social violence was a watershed event in the lives of millions of American lesbians and gay men. Beginning with Stonewall, an isolated and stigmatized group of individuals transformed themselves into a vital and influential political movement. In the process, our society's views of homosexuality evolved from being a shameful personal problem that no one would talk about, to becoming a controversial social issue, debated on TV talk shows, in newspaper columns, and at dinner tables across America. (Weiss & Schiller, 1988, 6)

The raid on the Stonewall Bar that night sent a stunning message to lesbians and gay men around the United States. As a result of this singular event—that occurred on the heels of the civil rights movement of the 1960s—Gay Liberation Front groups sprang up on university campuses across the nation. Marcus (1992) documented the role and involvement of college students and the importance of their challenges to their administrations. Sexual orientation issues finally made their way into the realm of education.

Homosexuality has often been explained as "a genetic defect, a mental disorder, or a learning disability" (Harbeck, 1992a, 1) as advanced by early scientific theories. In 1957, however, Evelyn Hooker published a study that showed no significant difference in the psychological adjustment of homosexual men when compared to a similar population of heterosexual men. Because further research by others demonstrated similar findings, the American Psychiatric Association removed homosexuality as a diagnostic mental disorder in 1973. In 1975, the American Psychological Association followed suit and also issued a statement to its membership that mental health providers must actively stop discrimination against lesbians and gay men. Concurrently in 1975, the National Education Association added *sexual orientation* to its non-discrimination policy. In fact, more than 200 professional organizations, including the American Educational Research Association, the American Federation of Teachers, the American Counseling Association, and the National Association of Social Workers, did the same (Harbeck, 1992b; Khayatt, 1992; Mayer, 1993; Pollack & Schwartz, 1995; Sears, 1992a). The National Council for the Accreditation of Teacher Education (NCATE) revised its standards for institutions seeking accreditation: NCATE now requires institutions to recruit, admit, and retain a culturally diverse faculty and student body. As noted by Sears (1995), this standard for diversity includes sexual orientation.

In 1998, the American Psychiatric Association, the American Psychological Association, the National Association of Social Workers, and the American Academy of Pediatrics adopted position statements and policies that oppose reparative conversion therapy—the attempt to make homosexual people heterosexual through various types of psychological and religious therapies. The American Psychiatric Association said there is no "scientific evidence that such therapy is effective; however, there is evidence that it is harmful" (Katz, 1998).

Despite these statements of nondiscrimination and opposition to reparative therapy by national professional organizations, Harbeck (1992a) noted that everyday life has not change dramatically. She stated that given the historical context, many lesbian or gay educators "remain invisible rather than face the harsh consequences of the previously almost unrestricted power of educational administrators and the extremes of community intolerance." Most lesbian and gay teachers remain invisible because of threats or experiences of hostility or "internalized oppression that leads to self-doubts and fear" (Harbeck, 1992a, 2).

Brief histories of lesbian and gay people in American education (Harbeck, 1992b; Khayatt, 1992; Mayer, 1993; Sedgewick, 1990) suggest that not challenging the status quo and remaining cloaked in invisibility are the usual and typical responses of lesbian and gay teachers who might face personal danger and financial loss if they reveal their sexual orientation. However, by 1992, based on cases that have been won in the courts, Harbeck (1992b) documented that lesbian and gay teachers nationwide have more latitude in being open about their sexual orientation. Although there is less danger of overt discrimination and job termination based solely on sexual orientation in some areas of the country, there remains the "real possibility of insidious incidents relating to limited advancement, ungranted tenure, mundane duty assignments, and undesirable teaching loads" (Harbeck, 1992b, 131). This state of affairs remains intact today (Karen Harbeck, personal communication, March 14, 1996).

LAWS AFFECTING TEACHERS

Dressler (1985) emphatically stated that "the law has been no friend to gay people" (599). He noted that the anxiety felt by society toward lesbian and gay people in general is heightened dramatically when discussion includes lesbian and gay people as educators.

The editors of the *Harvard Law Review* (1990) described societal attitudes toward lesbians and gay men as generally falling within four competing conceptions of sexual identity: the sin perspective, which views homosexuality as both negative and immoral; the illness perspective, which views homosexuality as negative and curable; the neutral perspective, which views homosexuality as a difference from which one should not experience discrimination; and the special construct perspective, which rejects categorizing people by sexual orientation and does not view homosexual acts any differently than heterosexual acts. These four conceptions drive the laws and policies that underlie statutes and regulations regarding sexual orientation issues. *Harvard Law Review* editors concluded that from past and recent historical views, and due to the increased attention directed toward lesbian and gay people in the last decade, gay and lesbian teachers receive mixed messages regarding the safety of being out of the closet in education.

Teachers have been sanctioned or dismissed across the country for a wide range of behaviors connected to sexual orientation, including convictions under sodomy or solicitation statutes, public homosexual displays, unauthorized comments made in the classroom regarding homosexuality, and private declarations of homosexual orientation. (*Harvard Law Review*, 1990, 85)

Although, in theory, teachers and other public employees retain their rights of free speech under the First Amendment, the Supreme Court has upheld varying levels of restricted freedom of speech for teachers in general and for lesbian and gay teachers specifically (Schneider-Vogel, 1986). Schneider-Vogel concluded that as a result, it has become nearly impossible to win challenges to employment dismissal based on freedom of speech grounds.

The editors of the Harvard Law Review (1990), Schneider-Vogel (1986), and Harbeck (1992b) offer common descriptions of cases involving gay and lesbian teachers, Following are the most notable:

• *Rowland v. Mad River Local School District*, (730 F. 2d 444, 6th Cit. 1984, cert. denied, 470 U.S. 1009, 1985): A female guidance counselor revealed her bisexual orientation to a colleague. The courts held that the employer could transfer her to a position that did not require student contact.

- *Acanfora v. Board of Education of Montgomery County,* (491 F. 2d 498, 4th Dir., 1974): Failure to include former membership in a gay organization in college on an employment application was upheld to constitute misrepresentation and was therefore grounds for dismissal.
- *Gaylord v. Tacoma School District,* (88 Wash. 2d 286, 559 P. 2d 1340, cert. denied, 434 U.S. 879, 1977): "The Washington Supreme Court applied [an 'inappropriate'] role model theory to uphold the dismissal of a teacher for immorality based on his status as a 'publicly known homosexual'" (*Harvard Law Review,* 1990, 91). The primary problem with the role model theory described in Gaylord was that sexual orientation was mistaken for sexual behavior.
- *Morrison v. California State Board of Education,* (1 Cal. 3d 214, 461 P. 2d 375, 83 Cal. Rptr 175, 1969): In this landmark case, the California Supreme Court decided that simply being lesbian or gay was insufficient grounds for dismissal unless inappropriate behavior could be documented.

The editors of the *Harvard Law Review* (1990) offered this admonishment:

School authorities must consider more than their conception of "appropriateness" in employing faculty members; their policies and attitudes toward any minority group or minority viewpoint instruct students of the viability of First Amendment protections and of the constitutional principles being taught. If gay and lesbian teachers are summarily excluded or stigmatized in the school systems, such disregard for the fundamental principles of fairness and equal protection mandated by the Constitution would teach students to "discount" important principles of our government as mere platitudes. (93)

The editors of the *Harvard Law Review* (1990) and Schneider-Vogel (1986) also discussed issues of equal protection under the Fourteenth Amendment. "Because the Supreme Court has declined to define sexual orientation as a suspect classification, discrimination against gay and lesbian teachers remains invisible" (*Harvard Law Review,* 1990, 92). The failure of the Employment Non-Discrimination Act (ENDA) to pass in the U.S. Senate in September of 1996 (S. 2056, 104th Cong., 2d sess., 1996) gave more recent validation that invisibility in the workplace is the publicly desired norm of the day. ENDA would have federally prohibited discrimination based on sexual orientation in employment.

Gains have recently occurred which may provide legal protection for lesbian and gay teachers and students in the future. On May 20, 1996, the United States Supreme Court overturned Colorado's Amendment Two because it violated equal protection under the law by singling out lesbians and gay men as a class of people. The Supreme Court ruling ensured

that states could not pass laws to deny lesbian and gay people equal access to the democratic process (Elizabeth Birch, Executive Director,
Human Rights Campaign, Washington, D.C., press release, May 20,
1996). In July 1996, the 7th Circuit Court of Appeals affirmed the case
of *Nabozny v. Podlesny* (1996) where a student in Ashland, Wisconsin,
sued the school district because it failed to protect Jamie Nabozny from
anti-gay harassment and assault. In May of 1999, the U.S. Supreme
Court ruled that school districts "may be held liable in cases involving
extensive sexual harassment of students by one another" (Boxall & Noriyuki, 1999, A1). Harassment of students based on sexual orientation is
indeed a form of sexual harassment.

The need for diverse role models and for examples of tolerance in the
classroom must be considered by school systems and the courts for full
consideration and inclusion of all people, regardless of sexual orientation
(Pope, 1995). However, some lesbian and gay teachers live in fear based
on litigation history in this country; they perceive that they are not safe to
reveal their sexual orientation.

Litigation seems to originate with students and their parents and with
school boards, but not with teachers. Harbeck (1992b) noted that teachers
rarely initiate litigation because most lesbian and gay teachers resign before facing the embarrassment of dealing with charges related to their
sexual orientation. She suggested, however, that since litigation is very
expensive for most school districts, lesbian and gay teachers would be
better positioned to maintain their jobs if they were willing to start the
litigation process. Although both the American Federation of Teachers
and the National Education Association provide legal support for teachers in these cases, Harbeck noted, few teachers choose to fight.

Despite the fact that 10 states provide legal written job protection for
lesbian and gay people, Woog (1995, 23) noted that gay and lesbian
teachers do not feel safe in schools. He acknowledged that "in all fifty
states, teachers who come out in the workplace—whether to their supervisors, colleagues, selected students, or the school as a whole—may be
regarded with suspicion, distrust, even downright fear." Woog's account
reiterates that Florida is not one of the states that provides legal written
protection for its educators.

LESBIAN AND GAY TEACHERS IN FLORIDA AND
NORTHEAST FLORIDA

Historical and legal precedent fuel the reasons why lesbian and gay
teachers may choose to remain invisible in northeast Florida. Sears
(1991, 1992b) commented that people in the South, more than in other

areas of the United States, continue to view homophobia as a socially acceptable attitude. Such an attitude encourages silence among lesbian and gay people in general and lesbian and gay educators specifically (Sears, 1992b). In Sears's view, the South is "a lonely place for a boy or girl blossoming into adulthood as a lesbian, bisexual, or gay man" (61). Florida's recent history supports this description.

The Johns Committee

On March 17, 1964, the Florida Legislative Investigative (sometimes interchanged with Investigation) Committee, chaired by (former acting governor) Senator Charley E. Johns of Starke, published a report entitled *Homosexuality and Citizenship in Florida* (1964). The purpose of the Florida Legislative Investigative Committee, established in 1956 and nicknamed the Johns Committee, was initially to investigate the Florida chapter of the National Association for the Advancement of Colored People (NAACP). Soon, however, it changed its focus to identify methods to detect and remove lesbian or gay individuals from Florida's schools and other state-funded agencies (Harbeck, 1997; Sears, 1997). Public school teachers and college professors were the primary targets of this investigation, as documented in the committee's report. Many teachers—some of whom were gay and some of whom were perceived to be gay—were publicly named and forced to resign. As Sears (1997) noted, the Johns Committee began an "8-year campaign, wrecking careers, and destroying families." Suicides of individuals involved in this public exposure are believed to have been in direct response to the public humiliation and disgrace (Pendleton, 1993).

Sears documented the voices of those who survived the Johns Committee rampage. One educator said, "Tenure didn't mean a goddam thing. If they wanted to get rid of you they would find a way. And they did" (1997, 81). A female educator added, "People were told that they were under suspicion because of their [single] marital status. Now, [30 years later] those women still live in fear" (106).

When the Johns Committee report, *Homosexuality and Citizenship in Florida* was presented to the Florida legislature in March 1964, it was called "disturbing," "crude," and "in bad taste." The legislature, while it continued to be repressive toward lesbian and gay people, discontinued funding for the Johns Committee (Sears, 1997).

John Evans, the day-to-day director of the now-disbanded Johns Committee, spoke to the Florida Federation of Women's Clubs in Jacksonville in mid-1964.

He warned that homosexuality was still flourishing in Florida educational institutions, with allegations of homosexuality and references to 123 individuals then, and presumably now, teaching in Florida schools. (Sears, 1997, 998)

The Influence of Anita Bryant

In 1977, former Miss America Anita Bryant staged her "Save Our Children" campaign in Miami. She mounted a successful effort to repeal Dade County's new gay rights ordinance that prohibited discrimination against gay and lesbian people in employment and housing. The premise driving Bryant's efforts was that private schools, including Bryant's own church school, would be forced to hire lesbian or gay teachers if the ordinance remained intact (Duberman, 1991; Harbeck, 1992b; Marcus, 1992). As a result of Bryant's success in Miami, the 1977 Florida Legislature produced Florida's anti-gay adoption law which discriminated directly against lesbians and gay men by ruling that "no person eligible to adopt may adopt if that person is homosexual" (Florida Statutes, 1995d). Ironically, to that date no openly homosexual person had attempted to adopt a child. Senator Don Chamberlin of Tampa responded to the proposed law with an emotional appeal to the Florida Senate during that legislative session.

The popularity of Archie Bunker seems to tell us that individuals in society need a relief valve. They need to express their prejudices and sometimes even to act upon them. Do we discriminate by state policy? Will the Florida Senate crush their spirit as all discrimination does? Will you try to identify, and magnify, and stigmatize? (Journal of the Senate, 1977b, 370–371)

Senator Lori Wilson also made a plea that fell on deaf ears.

The good old boys in Southern politics refused to give up their slaves until the rest of the nation whipped them on the battlefields. The good old boys refused to approve the 19th amendment granting women the right to vote until the rest of the nation whipped them in the legislative halls elsewhere across this land. The good old boys fought the 1964 Civil Rights Act down to their last ax handles until the rest of this nation whipped them in the courtrooms and on the streets and at the polls. And now, on the last remaining issue of human rights, civil rights, people rights, and equal rights, the good old boys are summoning all their remaining but weakening power for one last hurrah. Wouldn't it be nice when America reaches its destination if we were able to stand up and shout: Because of us, because of us, not in spite of us, but because of us, because of this Senate, because of this South, this country stands united on one more human and decent and fair thing? In closing, my fellow Senators and my fellow Southerners, let me share with you a dream: I had a dream that a Southern boy could grow up to be president; I have a dream that our good old boys in the South can grow up to be men. (Journal of the Senate, 1977a, 145–146)

In spite of Senators Chamberlin's and Wilson's impassioned efforts, the law passed, and lesbian and gay people in Florida were prohibited from adopting children. Senator Chamberlin was not re-elected; Senator Wilson did not run for office again.

The Bush-Trask Amendment

In 1981, Representative Tom "Reverend" Bush (of no apparent connection to former U.S. President George Bush) of Ft. Lauderdale and Senator Alan Trask of Winter Haven created the so-called Bush-Trask amendment (Florida Statutes, 1981) that carried anti-gay bigotry in Florida's history of higher education to a new low.

Bush stated that he resented taxpayers' money going to support such "garbage" as campus gay groups. When Rep. Joe Kershaw inquired if gays were not taxpayers, too, Bush replied that while they might be, so are "murderers, thieves, and rapists." (*The Weekly News*, May 20, 1981, 12)

Originally designed specifically to target homosexuality—both issues and people—in higher education, the Bush-Trask amendment was broadened to include all unmarried people, and would deny funding—including funding for athletics and student financial aid—to any Florida university that advocated sexual activity between unmarried adults:

No funds appropriated herein shall be used to finance any state-supported public or private postsecondary educational institution that charters or gives official recognition or knowingly gives assistance to or provides meeting facilities for any group or organization that recommends or advocates sexual relations between persons not married to each other. Sexual relations mean contact with sexual organs of one person by the body of another person for sexual gratification. Any postsecondary educational institution found in violation of this provision shall have all state funds withheld until that institution is again in compliance with the law. No state financial aid shall be given to students enrolled at any postsecondary educational institution located in Florida that is in violation of this provision. (Florida Statutes, 1981, 645–647)

Representative Bush appeared on the Phil Donohue Show in December 1980 to explain that this amendment was specifically targeting homosexuality in Florida's universities. He said of people who associated with Florida's lesbian and gay community: "If you lie with dogs you're going to get fleas" (*The Weekly News*, December 28, 1980, 1). Florida's

lesbian and gay civil rights organization, the Florida Task Force (FTF)—
of which I was executive director and lobbyist—issued a statewide call
for flea collars to be given to Representative Bush on the opening day of
the 1981 Florida legislative session. Hundreds of flea collars, many taste-
fully and some distastefully decorated, arrived from every area of the
state and were presented to Bush with great media aplomb.

The Bush-Trask amendment was attached to the 1981 Florida Appropriations Bill. Since line-item vetoes by a governor were prohibited in
Florida at that time, the Appropriations Bill with the Bush-Trask
amendment was signed into law by then governor Bob Graham. Upon
challenge by the Florida Department of Education, the Florida Supreme
Court unanimously found the Bush-Trask amendment to be unconstitutional. The Supreme Court judges opined:

The history of the interpretation of the First Amendment shows a steady movement toward protecting the free-speech rights of persons of all political and
moral views. Ours is a nation rich in diversity, and our strength has been in our
practice of allowing free play to the marketplace of ideas. We consist of many
divergent association groups, and as to each group there are sectors of the community to whom its values are anathema. Nevertheless, to permit the continued
building of our politics and culture, and to assure self-fulfillment for each individual, our people are guaranteed the right to express any thoughts, free from
government censorship. (Florida Supreme Court, 1982, 11–12)

Bush was not re-elected. Trask resigned his Senate seat in disgrace
when he was charged with seven counts of violating Senate ethics rules,
including numerous federal violations (*The Weekly News*, June 16, 1982,
1, 8).

The overturning of the Bush-Trask amendment was a major victory
for Florida's universities, teachers, and students, gay and non-gay alike.
However, it offered no protection nor did it lessen the possibilities that
lesbian and gay teachers would be removed from their teaching positions
if their sexual orientations were to become known.

University Nondiscrimination Policies

In 1994, the University of South Florida (USF) in Tampa and Florida
International University in Miami were forced by the Florida Board of
Regents—the governing body of the Florida State University System
(SUS)—to remove the term *sexual orientation* from their nondiscrimination policies (Simmons, 1995). Examination of the nondiscrimination
policies at the other higher education institutions in Florida revealed that
none included this term. In November 1995, the Faculty Senate at USF

became the first faculty group in Florida to publicly support enacting policies that prohibit discrimination based on sexual orientation (USF, 1995).

In 1998, following the murder of Mathew Shepard, a gay University of Wyoming student who was killed because of his sexual orientation (O'Brien & Rohr, 1998), the president of the University of South Florida (USF) requested that *sexual orientation* be included in the Board of Regents' official policies. She also asked—should the Regents choose not to include such language—if USF may adopt its own policy language protecting people on the basis of sexual orientation. The Board of Regents decided that it had no legal authority to add *sexual orientation* to the SUS's anti-discrimination policy (Gold, 1999). The chancellor indicated that he has "personal and religious problems" with adding such language to the SUS policies. In addition, he said that SUS policies must not provide more expansive protection that the state's non-discrimination policy which currently does not include *sexual orientation*. According to the language in the Florida Employment Policy (Florida Statutes, 1995e) and the Florida Civil Rights Act (Florida Statutes, 1995f), educators and employees in Florida still—in 1999—have no legal protection from discrimination based on sexual orientation.

Northeast Florida Schools and the Christian Coalition

In 1981, Jerry Falwell selected Jacksonville, Florida, in northeast Florida, as a test market for his Moral Majority membership campaign. He mass-mailed a ballot throughout the northeast Florida area. One of the questions on the ballot was, "Do you want a soliciting practicing homosexual to be allowed to teach your children in the classroom?" (*The Weekly News*, Sept. 23, 1981, 1).

A review of the nondiscrimination policies of the school boards in the five counties of northeast Florida—Baker, Clay, Duval, Nassau, and St. John—revealed that none offer employment protection for gay and lesbian employees, nor do they allow homosexuality to be discussed in any context within the public school system. Additionally, Clay, St. Johns, and Duval Counties have school board members who publicly identify with the Christian Coalition (Saunders, 1995).

Friedman and Downey (1994) noted a connection between the zealous fundamentalism of the Christian Coalition and other groups with similar anti-gay attitudes. Provenzo (1990, 71) spoke of the attitudes of these groups toward gay and lesbian teachers:

The ultra-fundamentalists consider homosexual teachers to be unfit to work with children. No consideration is given to the teacher's rights. It is assumed that if they are gay that they will try to influence the children they teach to follow their own sexual preferences. Rejecting the notion that the homosexual community can exercise its sexual preference, and let others do as they see fit, ultra-fundamentalist leaders believe that the homosexual community is interested in recruiting the minds and beliefs systems of American youth.

As a result, the active presence of the Christian Coalition in northeast Florida has likely influenced lesbian and gay teachers to burrow deeper into the darkness of their closets as they seek the safe but paranoia-producing confines of secrecy. Silin (1992, 15) referred to this phenomenon as a "moral panic which serves to reinforce normative sexual stereotypes."

Perpetuating the Fear

Recent incidences have served to validate and reinforce the secrecy. In 1996, WFSJ, a popular soft jazz radio station in Jacksonville, owned by Paxson Communications, refused to allow the Jacksonville Gay Chorus to use the word *gay* on the radio for fear that some listeners might be offended (Charisse, 1996). In 1997, gay-related books were kept out of the Brevard County, Florida, library (ChannelQ, 1998). Also in 1997, the Southern Baptist Convention called for a boycott of the Walt Disney Company because it enacted domestic partner benefits for lesbian and gay employees, and because it allowed Ellen Morgan to come out as a lesbian on the television situation comedy *Ellen*. The 1997 Florida legislature approved a ban on same-sex marriage (ACLU, 1997a), and also upheld Florida's anti-gay adoption law (ACLU, 1997b). In 1998, the Southern Baptist Convention struck again by issuing bizarre anti-gay resolutions (Human Rights Campaign, 1998), while Christian Coalition founder Pat Robertson warned Orlando of hurricanes, tornadoes, and meteors for allowing gay pride day to be celebrated in the city. In 1998, the ACLU filed a lawsuit against the Duval County School Board because of the School Board's practice of allowing prayer in schools and at school commencements; in May of 1999, a Federal Appeals Court found the School Board's actions unconstitutional by ignoring both the law and the requirements of separation of church and state (ACLU, 1999).

Incidences such as these remind teachers and others that their fears of discovery are founded in reality. Despite such gains in Florida as the inclusion of *sexual orientation* in the nondiscrimination policies in the cities of Key West, Miami Beach, and Gainesville, and the counties of Dade, Palm Beach and Broward, the bigotry and the losses in the de-

scribed situations serve to keep lesbian and gay teachers hidden and silenced.

Chapter 3

Methodology: The Participants and the Process

This study was designed to learn how the experiences of lesbian and gay teachers affect their roles in the education process. Three questions shaped the research project: How did these teachers interpret their professional worlds? How did they live their lives as lesbian and gay people? How did they work as lesbian and gay teachers in northeast Florida? Rubin and Rubin (1995, 1) stated that qualitative interviewing is a "great adventure" that illuminates new information. The use of this methodology extended the concept of the great adventure to this group of people whose voices and stories had not yet been heard by others.

THE USE OF QUALITATIVE METHODOLOGY TO INTERVIEW LESBIAN AND GAY EDUCATORS

The interview in qualitative research is a process that generates large amounts of data quickly and allows for immediate clarification and follow-up (Marshall & Rossman, 1995). This approach recognizes complexity and encourages participants to describe the world as they see it and live it. The interview process provided an excellent vehicle for encouraging participants in this study to express thoughts, feelings, perceptions, beliefs, and emotions about specific areas of research interest (Eichelberger, 1989; Merton, Fiske, & Kendall, 1990).

After a general discussion of the main topics for examination, the participants responded to particular questions (Rubin & Rubin, 1995) that were designed to discover how issues of sexual orientation influenced them and their work as educators, and how their life experiences related to their sexual orientation. The flexibility of open-ended, in-depth interviewing contributed to the strength of this research approach (Murphy, 1980). Surveys, questionnaires, or other research methods typically do not allow for the same level of flexibility, depth of information, and exploration of a variety of viewpoints, and were not utilized.

Interview studies attempt to examine research questions focused on how people understand and interpret their worlds. Their perceptions as revealed in talk become the raw data for study. Interviews provide "empirical data about the lives of people in specific situations and allow us to see alternate realities and modify our culture-bound theories of human behavior" (Spradley, 1979, 13). Both Murphy (1980) and Merriam (1988) noted that open-ended, free-flowing interviews are useful when observation will not provide the opportunity to see how people interpret their world, and when detail is desired.

Marshall and Rossman (1995) stated that research should build knowledge and explore the unknown. The interview questions for this work were designed to accomplish these research goals by focusing on the experiences of lesbian and gay educators in northeast Florida. Murphy (1980, 91) noted that "good [interview] questions are ordered, worded, and asked so that they provoke the [participant] to respond honestly and completely, often going beyond what he [or she] intended to say." Questions are probes, used to dig further for detail, and used in the search for understanding, clarification, elaboration, and encouragement. The interview questions for this study were designed for several purposes—to initiate the interview, to explore experiences, to provoke and probe, and to seek the meanings of those experiences for each participant.

Questions elicit information about unobservable experiences or behaviors: They seek opinion, values, desires, thoughts, and feelings; they attempt to learn what the participants consider factual; they determine stimuli to which the participant is sensitive; and they seek background and demographic information (Patton, 1990). Spradley (1979) favored descriptive questions that sought to reveal the language and culture of the participant. Patton's and Spradley's guidelines for structuring questions directed the development of the interview questions for this study.

The literature makes several recommendations about the conduct of interviews. For example, interviews should take place in settings that are natural and comfortable for the participants (Eisner, 1991; Marshall & Rossman, 1995). Any location where people feel safe and are willing to talk about their thoughts or feelings is appropriate (Eisner, 1991; Murphy, 1980). In this investigation, participants selected the interview sites, either in their own homes or at other meeting places in the northeast Florida area. The interviews varied from 90 minutes to 2 hours in length.

Such variation permitted the participants to use the time necessary to discuss their thoughts and experiences fully.

The interview sessions were audiotaped—with the tape recorder in full view of the participants—and then transcribed. Prior to the analysis of the material, each participant read her or his transcript and had the opportunity to edit the material for clarity, to add or delete information, and to ensure anonymity.

The word *I* is used to represent my positioning as researcher. Eisner (1991, 4) spoke of the researcher as "a human being and not some disembodied abstraction who is depersonalized." This method of giving voice to the researcher is one that Eisner exemplified in his own work. Therefore, where necessary for clarification, for emphasis, and for establishing context, the first person *I* will appear.

HOW NORTHEAST FLORIDA TEACHERS WERE SELECTED FOR THE STUDY

This study focused on the accounts shared by gay and lesbian teachers in the public school systems in the northeast Florida area. The geographic area of northeast Florida consists of the five northeastern counties of Baker, Clay, Duval, Nassau, and St. Johns. Three of the five counties border the southeastern Georgia state line. The city of Jacksonville, located in Duval County, is the urban hub of the region. According to the Jacksonville Chamber of Commerce (1999), the combined population of the five–county area is over 1,000,000. Each county has its own autonomous school district operated by elected school boards. The Duval County public school district, the largest of the five, has more than 6,900 public school teachers and 125,000 students.

The South has an on-going reputation of intolerance, although not all people who live there are politically conservative. The political climate in northeast Florida is neither welcoming toward nor tolerant of lesbian and gay teachers in the public school system. Sears (1991) described southerners as people who often reflect conservative values. He noted the enormous influence of the Southern Baptist Convention, with nearly 20,000 churches in the South. The headquarters of the Florida Baptist Convention is in Jacksonville. The First Baptist Church in Jacksonville— which seems to serve as a symbol of the fundamentalist religious phenomenon by participants in this study—boasts a congregation of more than 20,000 members in its downtown church alone (Interstate 95 billboard, Jacksonville, Florida, June 30, 1996).

Conservative Christian right-wing groups exploit peoples' fears about the well-being of families. Through their media and the pulpit, they perpetuate the myth of lesbian and gay people as child molesters "in spite of dozens of studies showing that between 95 and 98 percent of child sexual abusers are heterosexual men" (Kissen, 1996a, 78). Sears (1992a, 61) called the South the primary region of the country that "openly practices one of the few remaining forms of socially accepted bigotry—homopho-bia."

Further in-depth study of the terms *conservative, liberal,* and *toler-ance* could have been explored, as well as the foundation of the percep-tion of intolerance in the northeast Florida area and in the South. How-ever, given the nature and limitations of this study, such exploration would have been problematic, but the importance is noted and further research in this area is encouraged.

While 16 people were interviewed for this study, it is possible that other gay and lesbian teachers would have participated but did not do so for fear of identity discovery. This fear may have manifested in different ways. For example, Grayson (1987) noted that fear of exposure as well as fear of association kept people from participating in her study of les-bian and gay people. She added that some people, heterosexual and ho-mosexual alike, do not consider studies of lesbian and gay people or is-sues to be significant, and consequently discount such work. Madiha Khayatt, a lesbian and educator in Ontario, Canada, who researched les-bian teachers, revealed that some people were so fearful of her task that she was avoided by the lesbian community from then on (Khayatt, 1992).

It was difficult, therefore, to determine the number of people who could have made up the pool of participants; the number of lesbian and gay educators in the school system of northeast Florida is unknown. Not all are open about their sexual orientation, and not all who are so forth-coming are willing to discuss their sexual orientation with an outsider or a researcher. Therefore, the design of the study allowed the participation of all educators in the public school systems in northeast Florida who both volunteered and identified themselves as gay or lesbian. No partici-pant in this study identified bisexual or transgender.

Local lesbian and gay organizations provided means to make contact with some lesbian and gay teachers. Requests for participants appeared in local lesbian and gay media. The advertisements included the title and purpose of the research, a commitment to observe confidentiality, and avenues for responding to obtain further information and to schedule in-terviews. Word of mouth contacts and friendship networks were useful in reaching teachers who do not usually associate with the organized les-bian and gay community. Potential participants were invited to initiate a telephone call or an electronic mail message for further information re-garding this study.

Over the course of two months, 22 potential participants inquired about the study, 17 of whom agreed to be interviewed. Sixteen of the 17 teachers who initiated contact were actually interviewed. An appointment was made to meet one teacher in a location of his selection, but the teacher did not appear at the appointed time and place and did not make contact for rescheduling. Because of the provisions for anonymity, there existed no method to contact this or any other participant until we actually met face to face in the selected locations.

Ten participants learned of this project through the advertisements in the various gay community newsletters, while six heard about it by word of mouth. Fifteen interviews took place in participants' homes. One participant was interviewed in my home: Although the participant's biological children were aware of her sexual orientation, she stated she did not want her children to overhear our conversation.

THE PARTICIPANTS

At the time of the interview, each participant was a public school teacher in one of the five counties of northeast Florida. All appeared to be Caucasian. Ages ranged from 24 to 58, with a mean age of 39 years. Years devoted to teaching in northeast Florida ranged from 1 to 29, with a mean of 14. Twelve teachers were female, four were male. Eleven of the female participants identified as lesbian and one identified as gay. Three of the male participants identified as gay, while one identified as homosexual. All but one of the female participants had female domestic partners. None of the male participants had domestic partners at the time of the interview, although 2 of the men previously had partners in committed relationships that lasted 20 years or more each. One participant's partner died of AIDS-related complications; another's partner was murdered. Two participants were recipients of the Teacher of the Year Award. One of the two participants in this study who revealed being HIV-positive died of an AIDS-related illness several months before the completion of the study. Four individuals reported being active in their religious institutions and identified as having socially conservative views. One of the four described himself as being "ultra-conservative and proud of it." He was also the individual who identified himself as homosexual as opposed to the more socially accepted term *gay*.

Four individuals had partners present at the interview locations. Two of those partners were also teachers who agreed to be interviewed, one following her partner, and one in conjunction with her partner. There were no technical difficulties in interviewing two people at the same time. Both partners appeared to be as candid and as willing to share information as the other participants. It did, however, become challenging to separate the two individuals when transcribing the interview tapes, especially when a topic elicited excitement and they both talked at the same time.

Several teachers shared that they were thinking of leaving the field of education. As of this writing, 6 of the 16 participants are no longer teaching in northeast Florida. Two left Florida, one of whom is teaching in another state. Two retired. One quit. One died. Two teachers who are partners were considering moving to another state at the end of the academic year. As with participants in Kissen's work (1996a, 16), these educators found that acknowledging their lesbian or gay identity meant "rethinking the whole concept of being a teacher." For these participants, then, that concept of rethinking may have included deciding whether or not to remain a teacher in northeast Florida or to remain a teacher at all.

During the initial contact, participants received key information explaining that this inquiry required a tape-recorded interview; their names, the names of their schools and districts, and the specific grades they teach would not be identified in any manner in the study; and they would have the opportunity to review their transcripts prior to the analysis portion of the study to clarify material, assure anonymity, and provide further information if they desired. Finally, participants were reminded that there was no monetary reward or exchange as a result of participating in this study.

The names of the actual participants do not appear in any reporting or analysis of the data. Data from the participants were used generally as an aggregate rather than in a case-by-case discussion, although the transcripts of five participants appear intact in this work because I found their stories so poignant. The names that appear throughout this work and in the transcripts are names belonging not to participants but to members of my family of origin, all of whom live in California and Washington, none of whom are employed in the field of education.

Before the actual interviews began at the interview sites, the safeguards for confidentiality were reiterated. The participants then offered formal consent that was tape-recorded and later transcribed. Each participant also received a statement that offered assurance that she or he may withdraw from the study without penalty at any time either before, during, or after the interview.

Information gained from the participants may not be generalized to all gay and lesbian teachers. The selection method required that individuals be made aware of the study, self-select, then be willing to risk disclosure of their identity to a second party. Invitation efforts may not have reached deeply closeted gay and lesbian teachers because they may not be aware of or able to access local lesbian and gay literature and functions.

ETHICAL CONCERNS

Lee (1993, 2) defined sensitive research as that which sheds light on the uncomfortable or the unusual and may therefore assist in theory development because it challenges the "taken-for-granted ways of seeing the world." Problems with conducting research on sensitive topics include the potential effects on the participant's or researcher's personal life, as well as professional security. Both Lee (1993) and Troiden (1988) defined research on human sexuality in general, and homosexuality specifically, as being of a sensitive nature.

Therefore, because of the sensitive nature of this study, I had concerns that educators would not come forward to participate, yet 16 people agreed to be interviewed. When asked why they were willing to participate, their responses were similar: Each educator acknowledged that participation in this research was a way to help lesbian and gay students and other lesbian and gay teachers, without being identified and without losing or risking her or his job.

Like Woog (1995), I found that once participants began to share their stories, it was as if floodgates had opened. Nearly all expressed satisfaction with the fact that their concerns and experiences were being documented. In the words of one participant,

I didn't think anyone really cared about the way I felt or the fact that I have to keep hiding. I probably won't stop hiding, but my life has changed just by talking about it. Nobody ever asked how I felt about this before. Even I didn't know how I felt. I just stagnated through my career in pain.

All of the participants demanded anonymity because they feared job termination if their identities were discovered. Similar to Khayatt (1992), this study employed safeguards and precautions to protect participants from potential threat of identity discovery. In addition to the use of pseudonyms in reporting the study, the use of a regional geographical base consisting of multiple counties and school districts provided a safeguard against accidental or purposeful identification of participants, their schools, or the specific school districts in which they teach. These safeguards were clearly explained to each of the participants, who had the option of signing the letter of agreement with either her or his own name, with a pseudonym, or with an X. All participants in this study chose the X option. Additionally, participants had the opportunity to read the transcripts before their words were used here so they could personally insure that anonymity was not breached.

Participatory Consciousness

Heshusius (1994, 16) described the term *participatory consciousness* as "the awareness of a deeper level of kinship between the knower and the known," adding that such recognition of kinship—the seeing of self in one's participants—is an issue not only of obligation, but also of ethics. It is wanting only to understand and not to impose the self on the participants; however, it is also a process of not denying that self as researcher is present. As suggested by Heshusius, I attempted to forget my own ego concerns and be fully attentive to the participants, yet I was cognizant of my presence, my feelings, and my reactions.

Throughout the interview process and the writing of this work, I have been acutely aware that who I am as an open lesbian educator was central to how I approached this study. I acknowledged my presence in this study as a tool of research; I cannot pretend to be objective, so I was obligated to continually scrutinize my position. While I acknowledged my own participatory consciousness, great pains were taken to be careful with and respectful of the stories of the participants. My own career path demands that I be public about my sexual orientation; my bias is towards being out of the closet. For some people, however, being closeted may be a perfectly acceptable way of life. Therefore, I attempted to listen to the participants rather than impose my personal beliefs on them. I endeavored to listen and acknowledge through the personal filters that I brought into this work. The reader is invited and encouraged to see what I did not see in this population of lesbian and gay educators.

DATA ANALYSIS

The analysis of the data revealed an unfolding of information, some surprising and some expected. Identification of key words and phrases (Table 1) involved several strategies. First, concepts became significant because they were repeatedly present throughout the data and across at least several individuals. Second, on several occasions the participants themselves stressed ideas and marked these through their phraseology. Third, when concepts and ideas found in the extant literature appeared in the stories of the participants, these were identified as key. Finally, some concepts became significant because they appeared in the literature but were absent in the data. The identification of such key concepts led to the construction of themes that represented the participants' meaning of what it is like to be a gay or lesbian teacher in northeast Florida. Ultimately, the integration of these themes rendered complex and detailed interpretation of participants' meaning of their experiences.

Table 1
Key Words and Phrases Used in Coding

awareness of orientation	silence	laws
why become a teacher	peer relationships	Florida Department of Education
lesbian and gay community	colleague relationships	local school boards
culture of the community	relationship with parents of students	fear
culture of the school	relationship with students	self
climate of the school	spouse/partner	history
socializing	advocate for gay and lesbian youth	HIV/AIDS
lesbian and gay teachers	religion	recommendations
what is it like to be a lesbian or gay teacher in Northeast Florida?	harassment/ discrimination	allies/support
information transmission	changes in education	job satisfaction
feeling safe to reveal sexual orientation	personal definitions and labels	

Coding the Data

Initially, computer processing of the data seemed a useful approach for coding. However, Rubin & Rubin (1995, 241) noted,

the computer cannot do the creative part of coding, such as setting up and modifying the categories and figuring out in what categories each segment of the interview belongs. Nor can the computer label ideas as concepts or recognize themes, compare the separate concepts, find subtleties in meaning, or follow up comparisons or nuances.

Therefore, a commitment to the personal involvement required for data analysis and interpretation led to the decision to reject the use of computer programs for such purposes.

An early attempt to analyze the data began with the plan to use several levels of codes. At one level, the analysis yielded a grid approach to organization which connected themes and concepts to ideas, people, dates, feelings, and other categories. This level grouped like material and represented key constructs from the literature. However, the complexity of the data did not require such an intricate procedure, so this analysis strategy was discarded.

The selected procedure involved codes based on key words and phrases as participants generated information. The broad initial codes paralleled ideas found both in the literature and expressed in the responses to the interview questions. Subgroups of the broader codes reflected similarities and differences experienced by the participants to the same stimuli. Although all the participants, for example, expressed tremendous pain at having to hide who they are and who they love, each employed a variety of techniques to maintain the hiding behavior. Additionally, although each teacher expressed dedication to the vocation of teaching, nearly half voiced desires to leave the teaching field so they could be more open about their sexual identity. When such themes appeared in categories of the data, codes marked the associations.

Rubin and Rubin (1995, 229) stated that the purpose of data analysis "is to organize the interviews to present a narrative that explains what happened or provide a description of the norms and values that underlie cultural behavior." Concepts of Fine (1989), Harbeck (1992a), Kissen (1996a), and Pai (1990)—silence, fear of job loss, socialization, and culture—served as the raw material for constructing a theoretical screen through which to sift and analyze the data.

THEORETICAL FRAMEWORK FOR ANALYSIS

The theoretical framework used in the analysis and interpretation of the data in this study was based on key ideas extracted from the literature. The data were viewed and sifted through a theoretical screen both to affirm and expand upon extant theory. Theory is defined by Beauchamp (1968, 10, 12) as a "unification of phenomena within a set of events" with universal propositions and a "dimension of prediction." Theory, therefore, describes, predicts, and explains something. Its primary purpose is to explain events or phenomena. Beauchamp stated that the set of events which constitute a theory are the known, the assumed, and the unknown dimensions.

Although there are some known and some assumed dimensions about the professional experiences of gay and lesbian teachers in public schools through the works of Griffin (1992a, 1992b), Harbeck (1992a, 1992b, 1997), Jennings (1994), Juul and Repa (1993), Khayatt (1992), Kissen (1996a, 1996b), Mayer (1993), Olson (1987), Schneider-Vogel (1986), and Sears (1992b, 1997), the unknown dimension remains expansive. These studies involved educators who were open about their sexual orientation to some degree. Some were involved in gay-straight teachers' alliances—growing organizations in public schools where gay and lesbian teachers and their heterosexual allies come together to create a safe school environment—and some were active in the various gay- or lesbian-identified communities in which they lived. It was with these assumptions of openness and activism that this study began. It became apparent from the first interview, however, that these assumptions did not apply to this set of participants, these lesbian and gay educators in northeast Florida.

The participants' perceptions of the culture of the communities in which they lived and worked seemed to influence strongly their willingness to be open about their sexual orientation. Based on the interviews, participants appeared to reflect through three layers of culture: the school culture, the local-state culture, and the gay community culture. *Culture* is what people use to interpret their experiences and to generate their behaviors. It is the way in which people know and understand what to do through meanings and rules that are shared. The concept of culture also includes knowledge, skills, beliefs, and values that are transmitted from one generation to another (Bogden & Biklen, 1992; Geertz, 1973; Pai, 1990; Rubin & Rubin, 1995; Spradley, 1979). Culture defines who belongs to a group and who does not (Rubin & Rubin, 1995).

Pai (1990) noted that the cultural conditions of society affect personal and social modes of interaction in schools. Segments of U.S. society still adhere to the Puritan or traditional model of morality in spite of challenges to the validity of such values. Such a stance set many aspects of our culture in conflict with one another. As a result of the conflicting cultural conditions in northeast Florida, participants in this study felt that they must adhere to being silent about who they are and what they experience in the schools.

The concept of silence is often an effective tool to maintain the status quo (Fine, 1989). Fine (1989) noted that when individuals are silent, equal access is unobtainable, relationships are based on power, and projects of educational empowerment are undermined. Silence prohibits documentation. To the general community, silence implies that all is well; but to the silenced, it indicates the opposite. This study began to remove the cloak of silence that has long plagued these public school educators.

The review of the literature informed the research process used in this study. The need for an interviewer to cross boundaries in order to unmask the experiences of others is a concept drawn from the literature (Giroux, 1992). Because I am a lesbian, an educator, and known in the lesbian and gay community, such boundary crossing would not appear to raise any obvious issues. However, I am not a teacher in the public school system, nor am I secretive about my sexual orientation. It is likely, therefore, that boundaries indeed existed which may have prohibited potential participants from coming forward. As previously noted by both Grayson (1987) and Khayatt (1992), often a lesbian or gay person who is public about her or his sexual orientation is somehow threatening to those who remain closeted or secretive about theirs.

THE QUESTIONS: A PLAN FOR DATA COLLECTION

The principal means of data collection was the focused, in-depth interview. According to Seidman (1991, 69), "the basic structure of the interview is the question that establishes the focus." Seidman spoke of asking participants to tell a story because "everything said in an interview is a story" (64). Because not all people are comfortable with telling a story, the questions used in this study offered a sequential guide to sharing experiences and telling a story. The questions proceeded from a focus on the participants' self-discovery to the exploration of their viewpoints regarding what changes, if any, must take place within their professional settings. With these questions, there is a beginning, middle, and an end, a sequence that encourages the participants to share their experiences, reconstruct their histories, and tell their stories.

Participants were asked to share as much information as possible about their experiences, thoughts, feelings, history, and future in the context of their culture, knowledge, language, and employment. The questions or discussion items that follow served as initial starting points or guides, as suggested by Murphy (1980). They were designed to initiate conversation about specific topics and provided an inquisitive road map. Participants were encouraged to speak freely without interruption and with little interrogation. The narratives that developed as these teachers shared their stories comprised the data of the study.

The guiding questions were:

When did you become aware of your homosexual orientation? This question focused on whether the participants were aware of their homosexual identities prior to entering the field of education. In conjunction, I asked each participant whether he and she thought about his or her homosexual identity when making the decision to become a teacher. I also asked whether they were aware of risks associated with being a gay or lesbian teacher.

Describe the lesbian and gay community in northeast Florida. This discussion item focused on whether participants were aware of a gay and lesbian community outside of their immediate social groups and how they may or may not have envisioned themselves fitting into this community.

Describe the culture of the community in which you live. I wanted to know how participants perceived the culture of the general communities in which they lived. For example, did they see their communities as friendly, supportive, and safe, as harmful and frightening, or somewhere in-between?

How do you socialize in your community? Did participants socialize at their schools with colleagues, or perhaps with colleagues away from school? If so, how did such socialization occur? I was also curious about the nature of socialization within the lesbian and gay community in northeast Florida, as well as the nature of other arenas for the participants' social interactions.

Describe how you interact with other lesbian or gay teachers, whether or not they are in your school. This discussion item focused on whether participants were aware of other gay and lesbian educators in northeast Florida, and whether they had knowledge of a formal or informal support system through which educators could connect.

How do you think lesbian and gay teachers share information? I wanted to know how these educators get their information about being a lesbian or gay teacher in northeast Florida. How is culture transmitted among lesbian and gay teachers?

To what degree have you encountered harassment or discrimination in your role as a teacher? This question focused on whether the participants have ever experienced harassment perpetrated by colleagues, students, parents, or administrators, or if they are currently experiencing such difficulties.

What does it feel like to be silent about your sexual orientation? I asked participants how they experienced their silence and what role their own silence played within a climate of discrimination.

Do you think teachers in general—and you specifically—could be advocates for gay and lesbian youth? This question focused on whether participants believed teachers should be advocates and how the participants themselves could be advocates for lesbian and gay adolescents in general. It also explored whether participants believed they were role models and advocates for their own lesbian and gay students.

What changes, if any, must take place to allow for inclusion of lesbian and gay people in public education in northeast Florida? Participants were asked whether or not they had suggestions for change and whether they believed they were able to be agents for such change. Indeed, the participants often raised the issue of change. That is, given the nature of the content implicit in the research question itself and in the interview questions, the conversations inevitably led to discussions of policy and cultural change.

What is it like to be a lesbian or gay teacher in northeast Florida? This question begged the summary of the overall experiences of the participants in this study.

Each participant had the opportunity to review his or her transcript both for accuracy and for anonymity. While providing another step in assuring accuracy and honoring anonymity, this process was also heuristic. As Griffin (1992a) found in her studies of lesbian and gay educators, the reactions of the participants to their own words, thoughts, and feelings were unexpectedly powerful for them. One of the participants in this study commented, "This was an amazing thing for me, to read my words and to know I really exist."

The transcript review process led to very few changes by the participants. All agreed that anonymity was intact and that their stories were accurate. Several participants added further information to augment a point or two, but otherwise each participant confirmed that the transcripts as they appeared were accurate.

Chapter 4

The Silence Breaks: Voices of the Teachers

Although 16 people shared their stories—and portions from all 16 appear in subsequent chapters—I present here the near-intact transcripts of five people whose stories provided a great wealth of information about the unique experiences of being a gay or lesbian teacher. These stories touched me deeply, and informed this work—as well as my future work—in dramatic ways. One teacher, for example, hid from colleagues the fact that he was grieving the loss of his life partner who had been murdered because he was gay. Another man, who died before this work was completed, possessed tremendous internalized homophobia and anti-gay sentiments, yet he was the only participant who actually taught anything in the classroom resembling gay history. A female participant experienced what all the participants feared most: She had been accused of molesting a student. Another participant was so happy that someone asked about her experiences that she provided a chronology spanning more than 20 years. Finally, she and another participant talked about what it was like to have their partners teach in the same schools as they.

Although all 16 teachers said they chose to participate in this study as their contribution to create change for lesbian and gay people in northeast Florida, these five emphatically declared their desire to assist at the great risk of identity discovery. Therefore, the names—and occasionally the gender and pronouns—used in this study do not belong to the participants. All participants' names are actually names of members of my family of origin, all of whom live in California or Washington, as a means of maintaining anonymity. In addition, names of participants' schools and specific school districts were removed from the transcripts to further prevent identification.

It is with great awe and respect that I present their stories to you as they shared them with me.

BARRY

Barry is a pleasant man in his mid-50s. He holds two terminal degrees and was a priest for nearly a decade. He has been a teacher in the northeast Florida public school system for more than 20 years. Barry lives alone in an interesting and rather unusual house in a trendy, middle-class neighborhood. He spends much of his non-working hours participating in personal growth activities. Barry's voice is soft and gentle, calm and reflective.

Ronni: How long have you been a teacher?
Barry: Oh, 28 years altogether, 27 years in northeast Florida.
Ronni: Did you identify as being gay before you became a teacher?
Barry: I came out after I was a teacher, but I knew I was gay before I was a teacher. That's one thing that goes way back into childhood.
Ronni: What prompted you to become a teacher?
Barry: Ah, it's really weird. I needed a job. As soon as I got out of graduate school, a teaching job was offered to me. I intended to keep it a year and move on, but I ended up really liking it.
Ronni: What did you like about it?
Barry: I don't know. There just seemed to be a lot of satisfaction in it and a lot of excitement. It was a new thing. I knew nothing about it, so it was kind of like a brand new learning experience. I was learning along with the kids, and I really just got real involved in it; to see things that were happening with the youngsters were things that just excited me.
Ronni: What was your major in college?
Barry: I have a doctoral degree. That, by the way, was not by choice. I was a seminarian and I was required to go to school. I have a master's in elementary education and a master's in philosophy. I was in seminar for six years.
Ronni: Why did you go into the seminary?
Barry: Basically, it was something that was on my mind since I was about 11 or 12. It just kind of intrigued me. When I got into college—I went to a religious college—I became even more fascinated. It just turned out to be one of those things. This is where I want to be. Looking back on it now, I wonder if I wasn't hiding out from being gay, because a lot of us were.
Ronni: Do other teachers in your school know you're gay?

Barry: I'm sure most of them suspect. Probably quite a few. I'm sure word got out when my lover was killed.

Ronni: Do you feel like talking about that?

Barry: Yeah. The year my partner died was very, very difficult. When my partner was killed, that was a very difficult year—the circumstances under which he died and the pressure I was under, and the fact that my partner was gone. He had been missing for two days. They found his body on a Monday, and I didn't go back to school until the following Monday. I didn't dare share the information with anyone at school. They didn't know I was gay or know anything about the life we had together. Luckily, I had a family doctor who was able to get me out of school for a week. But it's like I had to walk into work as though nothing had happened. I had to grieve and hide at the same time. I didn't know what to do. It was extremely difficult. You just go through it, pretending as if nothing is wrong. My life-mate died and I had to pretend he never existed. That was several years ago. They still don't know at school.

I guess my first principal found out—I'm on my third principal— what was going on in my life and she was very supportive of me that year. One of the detectives I was working with for a couple of months after my partner was killed, his wife worked in my school. They told her what had happened so that basically she could get me covered. I knew I was going to have to go back to school pretending everything was fine. She literally pulled four teachers aside that I was good friends with. She gambled, she admitted later, but she took the chance and let them know what happened. None of those teachers are in the school anymore now, but I'm sure the word probably spread. So I think people know I'm gay, but I don't do much to encourage them.

Ronni: Oh, God.

Neither Barry nor I could hold back our tears. He continued to talk.

Barry: Had I not had the principal I had, I would have been fired. Not because I was gay, but because I didn't go to work. I missed, like, 60 days of work. I ended up in the hospital. I remember driving to work one day and looking up and seeing the exit sign on the interstate for Lake City. I had driven to Lake City, for God's sake! Fifty-five miles out of my way! When I got off the interstate, I sat there for 30 minutes. I didn't know what to do. It was like, okay, now what do I do?

The worst part was, I was going through each day pretending as if nothing was wrong. You go and do the best you can, but sometimes the best you can is not your personal best and you don't get the support you need. A friend of mine who is straight recently asked about my story in a support group. I explained about my partner, and the man just sat there with tears running down his face. He said, "That's the saddest thing I ever heard. If my wife were killed like that and I had to go to work, there would be all kinds of people supporting me. You had to turn around and work, and pretend."

It seems everything we do as gay people is unacceptable to the general population, but everything we do is a matter of survival. Lying becomes a norm for us because that's the way we cover. I remember one time, my partner and I had been together for about five years at the time. I was working on a project at the school administrative offices and there was a lot of evening work. I was considered to be the only single person on the project because they didn't know I was gay and didn't know I was in a relationship, and I couldn't tell them. I got elected to do all the evening work. When I complained about it, they said, "But you're single." I finally said, "That has absolutely nothing to do with it." I won the battle, but I kept thinking, "I am *not* single and this is putting a strain on my relationship." We gay teachers walk around pretending to be single. We are expected to go to social functions at work and drag along a date. I attend the functions and leave as fast as possible. It's such a real mental strain.

Ronni: Do you think students know you're gay?

Barry: I'm sure some former students have put two and two together over the years. At the age level I teach, and because I live on the other side of town—I've never taught where I live—they probably don't know. I'm still in touch with some kids I taught 28 years ago, but as far as actual students, I don't think so. I don't even think I've seen one of my kids on the street.

Ronni: In what ways do you feel you're affected by the institutionalized homophobia in northeast Florida?

Barry: Yeah, I'm very frustrated by it. For number one, I find I would like to be a lot more politically active than I am, and a lot of that has to do with job fears. I've only got a couple of more years to retirement in Florida. In the last year or two, things have been changing in my mind that I'd like to go back to the way I used to be in my late 20s and 30s, which was fairly politically active. I just don't feel comfortable doing it here in the South. It's funny. We went to the march (1993 Lesbian and Gay March on Washington) and a couple of us got our own tee shirts made. I would love to have seen everyone in the march dress appropriately for their professions or wear a sign for it. On the back of our shirts we put our names and our professions. I chose to put my first name and "teacher" under it. Being in the northeast Florida contingency, it was too risky for me to put more than just my first name. You don't know what's going to happen. It makes me feel a little on edge and a little leery, as well. I realize that in this country I shouldn't have fear. It's a political cause. Others did the same with their shirts. Actually, we probably should have dressed a la Malloy and walked quietly down the street. But if every gay and lesbian teacher in the country, or every gay nurse in the country, walked down the street, there would be masses of us shown to be in these professions. Let the drag queens come in drag if that's their profession. There's a spiritual sense and also some defiance to it.

Ronni: Do you provide resource information in your school?

Barry: Well, recently, I asked the principal if I could put up posters and applications around school for the (People With AIDS) Walk for Hope. So I did. A couple of days later they were down and I had to put more up. I had to do this several times because they apparently kept offending some people, but I just kept putting them back up and making the information available. The principal was fine with it. A couple of teachers even went to it. But that's about all.

Ronni: Have you gone to school functions where you've taken a partner?

Barry: No. I did take someone, though it was not a school function but school-related. One teacher who was a very good friend of mine had a son who was getting married last year. I asked if I could bring a date. My friend said yes, so I brought a male date. The teacher and family seemed to be okay with it. My principal was sitting behind me. He ended up leaving in the middle of the service because there was a (meditation-type) moment and he doesn't believe in that kind of thing. He started talking around school about this really weird wedding and was really bad-mouthing the teacher, so I confronted him with it. He said something to the effect that I didn't have a lot of room to talk because look at what I was there with. So I said, "Why, you want to make an issue of it, let's make an issue of it. What was I there with?" And he backed down.

Ronni: It sounds like you weren't afraid.

Barry: No, not then, I was not. A lot of this had to do with his personality. I've been very lucky with my last three principals. I don't make an issue of lifestyle, though. The principal I had prior to him—though I never made an issue of it and laid it at his feet—was very supportive of me at a time when I needed him to be without him ever saying anything to me. This one who went to the wedding was a strong personality, but he backed down. The new principal I have now is a very strong personality, but I don't believe he'd make an issue as long as I don't.

Ronni: Do teachers need more training in dealing with lesbian and gay issues?

Barry: Oh, most certainly! I'll give an example of some of the stuff that really irritates me. Teachers are very prone to stop any prejudicial language that they hear in school, unless it's prejudicial against the gay and lesbian community. A kid can call another kid *faggot* or *queer* and nothing is said. Or at the most, don't talk like that. But if they call them anything else, like a racial slur or anything like that, then they really deal with the problem. So it seems to be quite all right for kids to use that kind of language: *faggot, queer, dyke,* that kind of thing.

I had an incident where a youngster around 11 or 12 years old came into school, a fairly mature kid. For some reason, I don't know why, he told the class he was gay. I pulled him aside and told him, "You know, whether you are or not is not the point. You just opened yourself up to a lot of harassment." And I kind of let it go at that. Well, the next thing I knew, they had me, the principal, the kid's mother, the kid's aunt, and the guidance counselor all in the office. The concern of the school administration was not only what this kid said might be true, but that he needed therapy to cure him. And they asked, in essence, if I would support them. I said, "Absolutely not. I will not support you." I said, "I've spoken with the youngster. What I told him, and I was discrete, was that he's opening himself up to all kinds of trouble doing this. I don't think we should move in and help this child determine his sexuality. I believe it's already determined." Of course, I'm sitting there sweating bullets because the mother and the aunt are there. I said, "I personally don't believe that we or anyone else have the right to do that. What we need to do is support him and teach him how to cope with the world." The administration was getting very rattled by the whole situation. Suddenly, the mother spoke. She said, "I'd like to thank you. In my mind it doesn't make one bit of difference what my son is." She said, "I happen to have a gay brother. Whatever my son is, I want him to grow up to be a decent human being and be happy with himself." And she said to the rest, "You're totally wrong, you're crazy if you think I'm going to put my son into therapy to cure him." Well, then someone stupidly asked, "Have you checked to see if your brother has molested your son?" That just blew her to the ceiling! I just sat there grinning. In essence, she turned around and said she realized that her son may be a little young to be making such statements, but if that's the way it's going to be, that's the way it's going to be. She was going to support him rather than try to change him, and she liked my advice to the boy. If this is what you feel, this is not the time or place to spread it around. You'll get yourself beaten up.
Ronni: What a strong mom!
Barry: Yeah, I was really impressed.

I asked Barry if he was aware of the anti-harassment policy that included *sexual orientation* in the *Florida Code of Ethics and the Principles of Professional Practice in Education* brochure (Florida Statutes,

1995a, b). Like most of the teachers in this study, he was not aware of the policy or the brochure.

Ronni: Do teachers stop harassment against lesbian and gay students?
Barry: Well, see, it's really interesting because even in our profession where you think this stuff wouldn't take place, it's the same as the rest of the world. I heard a teacher mention not long ago, talking about so-and-so's son who's queerer than a three–dollar bill. I was right on the verge of saying something, but it wasn't worth the effort. It would have created more problems for me. The teacher and I weren't getting along anyway.
Ronni: Are there other lesbian or gay teachers in your school?
Barry: Well, two years ago, there were two gay men and four lesbians. Now, there is myself and two gay women. They're not out to me, but I know who they are. There is a community service officer who is a lesbian. And I have a lesbian substitute who comes in for me.
Ronni: Do you talk with those other gay teachers in your school?
Barry: No, but I occasionally run into them in restaurants.
Ronni: So you don't have a support system right now in school with other lesbian and gay teachers?
Barry: No.
Ronni: Is there any kind of support network available to you, say, through the union?
Barry: I really have no idea.
Ronni: Do you know about the national lesbian and gay organizations?
Barry: I know they exist, but I don't know about them. It would be nice if there was a support group for gay teachers in this city. I myself feel as if I've learned to cope with it, but actually that's not true. I am finding it tougher now than I used to.
Ronni: Why?
Barry: There was kind of a nervous aspect to the Walk for Hope, although I felt better about it when I saw straight people there. I was interviewed several months ago about when my partner was killed and I used a pseudonym, like we're doing here. But just recently in an article I allowed them to use my real name. There was a tension associated with it. The world isn't fair, and it's also unfair that we have to live with this tension.

I remember a year or so ago, when I was participating in a personal growth workshop. I was panic-stricken, just panic-stricken. I was having a real issue with what I call editing. I had to edit everything and felt so unfocused. Anyway, once the process was completed, the instruction was to hug everyone in the group. I said aloud, "Wait! I'm uncomfortable with this. I don't like hugging strangers and I don't want strangers hugging me." They asked if they could shake hands and I said, "Yeah."

When we were finished, a woman said to me, "I admire you so much. I have always wanted to do that but never had the nerve." And it was like, Bingo! At the next instructions to hug were the words "if you wish." Eight other people in the workshop chose not to hug! I gave myself permission, which gave them permission. I also decided in that workshop to quit editing my words and changing my pronouns just because of what people will think of me. I'm tired of it. I decided to be honest, to finally be me, and other participants benefited from it. I've not done a workshop since then without being totally honest. By the way, I am now the biggest hugger in northeast Florida. Want one?
Ronni: Yeah!

A lovely bear hug ensued—a gift from a gay man to a lesbian.

Ronni: A recurrent theme among those I've interviewed is that there is the frustration of being closeted, and the very deep frustration of not being able to help lesbian and gay students if they come to you for help.
Barry: I remember growing up as such a closeted teenager. Luckily, I was a busy and motivated teenager and kept issues out of my head. And I thought I was the only one. It's bad today, much worse, because kids know we're out there and we can't reach out to them or we'll lose our jobs.
Ronni: School counselors in a class I taught told me that even as counselors, if gay kids come to them there's nothing they can do.
Barry: Because teachers and counselors and everyone in northeast Florida has a mindset that says this is wrong, and if you help them, then you're encouraging them. And where *do* these people get the idea that kids can be changed? I have no idea. It's like they work with the notion that a homosexual orientation is a disorder or sin. If they've made the decision—as if it were a choice—to be gay, just unmake it. They think it's that simple.

When I think about it, I think I was 26 years old before I consciously found my first gay bar. I found it by accident and stumbled in. Up until that evening I tried consciously to not be what I knew I was. By the end of the evening I knew this is what it's all about. I was a kid in a candy shop. I went through adolescence all over again. I did everything by the book. About a year later I came out to my parents. My father was fine with it. My mother went right through the ceiling. Irish Catholics, you know. My father suggested counseling. He found me a psychiatrist and said it'll help my mother feel better if I go. Well, I thought, okay, I'll go and try to change to be heterosexual. The psychiatrist let me try this for about three months. Finally, one day he asked, "What's going on here?" I said, "This isn't working." He said, "Of course it's not working. What you need to do is learn to accept yourself. You don't need to worry about your mother accepting you. She does or she doesn't." Trying to change didn't work. Any strain we as gay people go through is coming to the realization that we are who we are.

Barry retired after 30 years of outstanding service as a public school teacher in northeast Florida.

BARBRA

Barbra and her partner share a Florida-style home in a suburban neighborhood. Both women are teachers in the public school system. Both describe themselves as extremely closeted. Barbra saw my ad in the *Out & About*, a local lesbian and gay newspaper. She telephoned several times to find out about this study. She shared that information with her partner and both agreed to be interviewed. Although the meeting with them took place in their home, they were interviewed separately. Both are 40-something and quite striking in appearance. Both Barbra and her partner have been in Florida for most of their lives.

Ronni: How do you identify yourself?
Barbra: In social situations with people like myself, I guess I use both the terms *lesbian* and *gay* to identify myself. But only in limited circumstances and situations, only when I'm with a limited group of people.
Ronni: How long have you been teaching?
Barbra: Nineteen years, all locally.
Ronni: When you went into teaching, did you know you were a lesbian?
Barbra: No, I wasn't out yet. I came out only four years ago. I was married twice. Then I met this person. We just clicked and that was that. It was interesting. We taught at the same school. I knew she was gay and I had a problem with it, not because of her, but because there were many kids at the time who were also gay, and because of my belief that there were three or four gay teachers at the time dealing with these kids. I was thinking they were imposing this on the kids. Of course, now I know that's crazy, but that's what I was thinking.
Ronni: Do you think other teachers and administrators think that?
Barbra: I don't know. I haven't really thought about it. Maybe. It's rough. Could be. I guess it's kind of natural for kids to be attracted to their teacher. For PE (pyshical education) coaches that stereotypically seems to be where a lot of gay people seem to concentrate in education.
Ronni: I remember looking back on my education. A PE teacher seemed to be more personal, had more one-on-one time with the kids than, say, the English teacher.

Barbra: You're right. It's because PE teachers have more time. I've taught both in the classroom and for a few years as a PE teacher. As a PE teacher, I had more time. The kids spend more time in the gym, and you have more time to hang around and chat with them. In the classroom, the bell rings and they come and go. You don't have the opportunity to spend time with them. No time even to breathe. I think that has a lot to do with why PE teachers seem more personal.

Ronni: What did it feel like when you were coming out?

Barbra: It was kind of strange because as I said, we were both in the same school. The school was small enough that you couldn't hide a lot from the faculty or the kids or whatever. I dealt with it the best I could. I said, "This is who I am," but it was strange.

Ronni: Did other people in school know?

Barbra: Probably. And people who knew my partner were fine with it. But there were her friends and there were my friends. My friends kept saying, "You know, you're getting into a situation where I don't think you want to be." It was kind of crazy. But most people just stood by and watched it happened and that was that. They didn't really say a lot. The kids, of course, kids are kids and they're going to talk no matter what you do. Nobody was ever mean. In fact, most people were very caring or concerned.

Ronni: Have you experienced any kind of discrimination at all?

Barbra: No, not towards me. But kids are cruel with each other. I've seen in the past two years that if a kid is different, it's automatic. "Oh, he's gay." Or, "She looks gay." Just this afternoon some girls were working on some things dealing with photos. They didn't want to use one because they thought a boy looked gay. They say these things without even thinking of the real meaning. It's just what they say.

Ronni: Are they ever stopped from using these words?

Barbra: I try to stop them. But I do different things with my kids because I have a different way of teaching and I can get away with different things because of what I teach. So I do that. I kind of ask them, "Why do you say that? What do you mean when you say that?" A lot of times they'll say, "Oh, I don't really mean that. That's just what we say." Sometimes they'll say, "Well, don't you think he's gay?" and I would say, "Well, why would you think that?" I just try to get them to think about what they've said. We talk a lot about stereotypes and stuff like that. Most of them will finally say, "Oh, yeah, well, that's a stereotype because of the way he [looks or dresses or talks]." I use *he* because that's what I heard more often. I can remember only one instance where girls talked about another girl when they thought she was gay.

Ronni: Are there gay kids in your school?

Barbra: Not that I know of. The only one I can think of was a senior boy about three years ago. We have one girl right now who probably is, but I don't know her that well. I'm only judging by who she hangs out with and how she looks and some of those things I've heard, but I don't really know.

Ronni: What would you do if a student came to you and said, "This is what I'm feeling. What should I do?"

Barbra: Unless it was a student that I felt really, really, really comfortable with, I'd send them to counseling.

Ronni: The rules seem to make it so volatile for teachers to talk with students about being gay. What students seem to say is that they won't talk to counselors because at the end of the day everyone will know about it. Have you had students ask about HIV or AIDS?

Barbra: Oh, yeah. We have to deal with HIV as part of the curriculum. We send home a document for parents to sign that says the students will be dealing with controversial issues including HIV. If the parents don't like that, they have the option to remove their kids during discussion of certain issues. But these kids have to know all of this. We bring in speakers all the time. Gay issues will come up and we deal with it.

Ronni: If a student were asking about sexual identity issues, would you refer her or him to JASMYN (Jacksonville Area Sexual Minority Youth Network)?

Barbra: No, I'd go through the school counselor. Well, I don't know. I could probably mention it. Yeah, I could do that discretely.

Ronni: Are you afraid of the school system learning of your sexual orientation?

Barbra: It's really frightening, but I'm more afraid of the students knowing. My principal actually knows. He knows both of us. He's known for a long time. He hired me knowing that. We have many gay teachers on our faculty. He has never indicated that was any kind of problem whatsoever. Maybe I would feel entirely different if I had another principal, if it was someone I didn't know and feel comfortable with. But that part doesn't bother me so much. It's more the kids, because they're the ones who can be mean, nasty, and do the damage.

Ronni: Have they been mean or nasty in other ways to you?

Barbra: No, never to me, but to each other. I don't put up with it. I have real high expectations, so I haven't had trouble with mean and nasty.

Ronni: What do you think the school system could do to make life easier, safer for lesbian and gay students?

Barbra: I don't know. I don't know. I don't have an answer to that. I don't know what they could do. A support group possibly. I suppose anything is possible. I don't know what the research shows will work, in that new rainbow curriculum, I don't know how it works. That might be an option, the curriculum in the younger grades. I don't know. This county is so scary, so backwards. I don't think such a curriculum could happen here.

Ronni: Do you think the inclusion of sexual orientation issues for in-services for teachers would be helpful?

Barbra: I don't know. Speaking from years of experience, most teachers are turned off by in-service of any kind. We've had some really bad in-services. But then again, if it catches you and you know there's some benefit, well, it depends on how it's handled. I doubt you could get it through, though.

Ronni: What about sexual orientation issues in teacher training course work and recertification courses?

Barbra: Now that would be helpful. That could work, even here. I think it would be great for education majors. The more they can see of what's going to happen in the real world when they get out of school is so good for them.

Ronni: Did you have questions about your own sexual orientation when you were a teenager?

Barbra: I didn't really question it until college, and even then I put it out of my mind. I really didn't deal with it until about four years ago. I didn't allow myself to have questions in college. I was supposed to have a boyfriend, so I did.

Ronni: Do you live near school?

Barbra: No. It's just not a good idea. I wouldn't care if you're gay, straight, whatever. I wouldn't want to live in the same area of town as my kids. Its just not a good idea. I know many people do it, but it's crazy. Kids are so nuts anyway. I remember going to the grocery store one time. One of my kids was a bag boy. Monday in school I heard about the beer I bought. Just because I'm your teacher doesn't make me a whole lot different than most people. I asked him if he had a problem if I have a beer or two when I'm home on Saturday night.

Some of the girls really caught me off guard the other day. They were eating lunch and I was trying to do something and I wasn't paying a whole lot of attention to them. They said, "What if we come to see you at your home? What are you like at home?" I was, like, excuse me? They really caught me off guard. They said, "Well, you're really more like our friend than our teacher so what if we just came over in the summer and we just sit and talk and that's all?" I said, "We'll cross that bridge when we get to it," or something. Goodness! But it kind of, and thinking back to when I taught at a private school, that was kind of something the kids expected basically. They thought of you more as their friend than their teacher. I was real surprised. It's been years since anyone ever mentioned that. That would be real, real tough. Things have changed so much. I used to throw a party on Saturday nights sometimes for the kids, but things have changed so much that there's no way now. We have to be so careful, even if it's just from liability perspective.

It's difficult. You really have to be careful. You really aren't even supposed to touch kids anymore, and it's tough. The black kids especially like to be touched, and they love to come back after graduation. It's different. Yeah, I even see it with speakers who come in and talk to the kids. They'll say, "Do you mind if I touch you?" They will tell the kids what they're doing, like, "This is the way someone started a fight and I'm going to shove you. Is that okay?" It's very neat.

I took some kids to the jail the other day. The juveniles go into juvenile population unless they start having problems, then they can ask to go into solitary. The question that sort of went unasked was, "How many of those guys are gay?"

I've been thinking about your question of if I knew any gay kids. Actually, it would be impossible for kids to come out in my school. They'd be crazy to come out. They'd get killed by their peers. We had a book to read in my class that talked about a young man who was living on the street and pimping, having survival sex. The kids in my class said all the awful things that the boy was experiencing was okay except for that. Why would he want to do that? They went on and on about behavior. Totally unforgiving. And it's the black kids who seem to be the most critical. White kids seem to be able to identify with some particular person, but the black kids don't seem to be able to do that.

Probably the strangest thing that happened while I was teaching was during my third year in a school with tough kids. We had a kid who was there one year as a male and came back the next year as a female. It was handled really well, especially by the principal. The student you knew as John came back as Jane. And since the kids were transitory in that school, they didn't know. I don't think he went through the actual surgical change but he definitely went with the hair and the dress and the makeup and all that.

I wonder what role in all this the First Baptist Church is playing. I grew up in that church, and it's scary to me. I used to teach gifted kids in junior high. I can remember a kid who made a statement, I don't even remember what we were talking about, and she made a statement that there are no gays in the First Baptist Church. No shit!

Barbra and her partner continue to teach in the public school system in northeast Florida. They plan to remain closeted until retirement.

LEN

Len and I had a mutual friend who thought Len would be an interesting participant for this study. I called Len and he invited me to his apartment where he lived by himself. He proudly told me that he was a lifelong resident of northeast Florida and a product of Florida's schools. Len was a tall man in his late 40s. His pale, thin appearance gave away his failing health, although Len referred to being HIV-positive only obliquely. He was quite chatty, strongly opinionated, and extremely pleasant. He struggled throughout his life with his gay identity on one hand and his deeply religious, anti-gay upbringing on the other. His story sometimes shocked and sometimes saddened me. Len sat in a recliner-type chair that he affectionately called his "womb." Len died from complications of AIDS shortly after he read and approved his transcript for this work. He did not live to see its completion.

Ronni: When did you know you were gay?
Len: I probably knew I was gay somewhere in junior high school because I had terrible crushes on a couple of the guys in my class. But being in a Catholic school, as I was all my life, such things were just not even thought about. When ideas changed about sex—personal sex and sex with other people—I guess that's when it was. I remember in high school having a dreaded horror of PE class for fear I was going to get an erection. Thank God it never happened.

There was a bookstore, well, a newsstand, downtown. The guy used to sell very primitive gay material. Somehow I discovered these magazines and started buying them. Of course, I never left them in the house. I always left them somewhere down the street.

I went to seminary for a year after high school and kind of thought I'd beaten it, if you will, to a certain extent, not to a total extent, but to a certain extent. Didn't work. I went to college, and it was in the summer of '69 that I met somebody on the beach in Jacksonville, someone who was here visiting relatives. Even then I wouldn't say I was out. I went back to school. I was in the monastery for six months, I guess. I met Brother John, who figured out from several things I said that I must be gay, and we had a small tryst. That's a cliché. But anyhow, he left, then I left for school about a week and a half later.

I came home and my mom said, "Why don't you see if there are jobs here in the county?" My degree is in a field where teachers are a dime a dozen, but luckily for me, God was smiling on me that day, I guess. Somebody saw my name and my experience and asked me to come in for an interview. That's when I started teaching here, 24 years ago.

When I moved back here—I remember when I was in high school seeing an ad in a paper for a place where homosexuals were—I took to cruising the streets like a damned fool. Sure enough, the streets were quite crowded in those days. I met somebody at the time with whom I had a very stormy four-and-a-half-year relationship. He was charming and would have done anything for me, but he had been out for a long time and I just came in the door, so to speak. This was probably 20, 23 years ago.

But I don't think I've ever come out to my parents. My dad found a letter that had been written to me or by me or something, I forgot what it was now, and confronted me, the summer of 1970, shortly before I left for the monastery. We made kind of a pact that we wouldn't talk about it to my mother. If he wouldn't tell her, I wouldn't tell her. I think my mother is finally now coming to the realization—it's a relatively new realization. She would use terms like *queer* and *faggot* about people. She was a secretary at a school here in northeast Florida, and she would talk about Mr. So-and-So not showing up for school the next day because he had been picked up at the park. Someone who taught at the school that she worked in died recently. She was very fond of him and she said, "He never did admit he was a homosexual and he never did admit he had AIDS." I said, "Well, wasn't that his prerogative, Mother, to live the life he wanted to live?" I wonder what she'll say about me?

So, as far as the classic definition of coming out, I mean, I'm not sure that I have. A lot of it is job-related, a lot of it is personal, I don't know. Religious, personal, whatever. The one thing I've always hated, if you'll pardon the expression, is screaming faggots. I feel no closer to them than I do to narrow-minded straight folks. I'm not at all opposed to telling them that I don't find them at all appealing. And I'm not an activist. I'm not one of those who've said to themselves, "You are one of many and we've got to come together, this and that, this and that." No, no, I don't believe that straight folks come together with rednecks to make their points valid. But, again, as far as a classic definition of coming out, I know who I am.

I would never say to anyone that I like what I am. I've never liked what I am. The people I know, I love them to death. Don't misunderstand me in that regard. I am not at all angry with them because they are and I am this thing. I'm sure that the friends I have are better than the friends I would have had in the straight life.

I've oftentimes thought God was good to me because while I'm a teacher, I don't like nor have the patience for babies. Yeah, I see them at church and I like them. Maybe it's just because I'm getting older and I know that. I know that my patience level at school is getting a lot less than it used to be. Then again, there are things I don't let bother me like they once did. I don't like insolence and I don't like impertinence, and I don't tolerate either one of them from the kids. But by the same token, there are things I let slide that I would never have let slide before. I've seen my standards in all the classes that I teach, from advanced placement to the honors kids to the standard kids, I've seen the standards slide terribly. Even then, I can't keep as many of them at the grade level I want, grade-wise. But if you don't make adjustments, too many kids fail. You'll feel bad. The administration looks askance at you. Though I've never been called on the carpet for bad grades, it's still a lingering idea out there.

We have a fellow who is retiring this year whose biggest problem is he's never been able to bend or change in any way. One of the things that's most irritating about it is that, okay, this is not the school you came to in 1959! This is not the school I came to in 1971. You've got to change and I've got to change, but he never would. In that regard, I try to hang onto as many standards as I can.

It's funny. There's this guy I see at church on Saturday nights. He was my high school history teacher. Last night I had this urge to jump up and tell him, "I was your student 30 years ago. I just want to tell you after all these years that I think you're the greatest teacher I ever had and one of the finest men I ever knew." I always said to myself that I hope I'm as good a teacher as he was. I knew I'd be great at what I did. I used to think about that myself, one of the rare places about my life where I felt good about myself. I knew I was a good teacher. In the last few years I'm not so sure I can feel that way. I think I'm good. A kid I taught years ago was substituting in my school. He said that all the things I did and all the harassment I gave him really paid off and he'd gotten his degree. The damnedest part about this profession is you have to wait at least five years for any kind of gratification.

Ronni: So did you talk to your former teacher?

Len: Yeah. I told him. Yeah, I guess even after 30 years it's nice to hear something nice about yourself. But again, it's like, for me to tell you in any way, shape, or form that I am happy with what I am, it would be a lie, okay? I'm happier now with myself than I've probably been in a long time. That's more religious than anything else. Growing up in a Catholic home with very good Catholic parents, going to Catholic schools from the fourth grade through college. In some people's minds I have hang-ups. But I don't consider them hang-ups. I love my church. I understand what my church is saying to me. I understand that if you're going to be a member of an organization as long as this organization has been around, well, maybe that's my little history, that the organization has rules. And if you don't follow those rules, you put yourself in opposition to the organization that you want to be a part of.

I've had two other relationships in my life, one of which was two-and-a-half years and stupidly blown apart by me and my vanity. The other was about five-and-a-half years. That ended because, again, there were psychological problems with me. As the relationship went on for as long as it did I thought I could live this way. Of course, it didn't work. It's interesting. He misses me now, but too bad.

I'm not really content with my life. Don't misunderstand me. I love to travel and I have the money to travel at this point after all these years. With me, this is it. What you see is what you get. I don't have all those problems that go with a house, and my car is 11 years old, God love it, and it drives as well as the first day I was in it. I'm one of those who basically doesn't buy anything unless he has to. My chair, my womb. I looked for a new one, but nothing materialized.

It will be a year in August sometime since I've been out to the bars. Part of that is physical. I can't go out and stay up late on a Saturday night and be able to get up and go to work on Monday. Or I could go to work on Monday, but by Wednesday I'd feel like I'd been hit by two trucks and a train. My philosophy has always been, if these people are going to pay me to do this work, by God, I'm going to give them 100%. But it's like as time marched on, and I didn't go out, I became more comfortable staying at home by myself.

Years ago, someone told me that you never get your meat and potatoes in the same store. Don't misunderstand me. I'm going to a 20–year reunion of the school where I teach this summer. There are two gentlemen, one of whom is probably fat and balding. But everyone knew, including them, that they were teacher's pets. They were so gorgeous and so attractive. But I never, never, ever, ever—even though I've seen them out at clubs and they've seen me—I've never, ever, ever, ever touched them or any student. Maybe it was subconscious or maybe even consciously, I admit I treated them somewhat differently due to the fact that they were not only handsome, but also charming.

Ronni: Are you talking about students you knew specifically to be gay?

Len: No! Oh no, no, no, no, no, just students who were adorable. There are some that I've been able to detect, but mostly I don't look for that.

Ronni: Do you think your students know you're gay?

Len: No. No, I don't think so, not anymore. I think because it's been a while since I've been out. The latest crop of new arrivals, I haven't seen them out because I don't go out. Also, when the drinking age was 18 it was difficult, because they'd turn 18 and show up at the bars. Things calmed down as soon as it went back to 21. I don't see them out and about. In that regard, well, a girl asked me—I don't remember how many years ago it was, time passes so quickly—but she said, "Are you gay?" I said, "Well, no, I'm happy but . . . ." You know, I was caught off guard because she said it in front of the whole blamed class. I don't know, well, I don't remember exactly how I handled it except, yeah, I'm a happy person, so. And that was the end of that. It was never brought up again. There have been other times a few years ago when I was with my partner. We went out. After he left, I went back out again, but I didn't see many students. I did see one or two current students, but what I did see were kids I taught several years ago. Surprised me, actually. I have lousy radar in that regard. Sure, sometimes you can see it or you might even hope in some perverse sort of way. But, even so, I pride myself on never, ever, ever having touched a kid. Never in the school. I don't think I swish (act effeminate). I don't feel there is any kind of knowledge about me. I certainly would not tell anybody. I've never told anyone at work.

Ronni: So your colleagues don't know?

Len: Well, I have one dear, dear friend who quit teaching last year in disgust who I think had a pretty good idea but, no, I've never come out and said to my colleagues, not any one of them.

Ronni: What about your principal?

Len: Heavenly days, no! There was one person who I almost did tell, but he turned out to be a total flake, so I'm thankful I didn't. That was many years ago. No, I never have. One of the women in my school may know, but we don't discuss it.

Ronni: Are there other gay teachers in your school?

Len: I really don't know. There's a guy who teaches right next door to me. I don't know if he's married or not. He never talks about it. I don't know. The rest of them that are there, in most cases, well, there's a PE teacher who I know is, but we don't broach the subject. There was another PE teacher years ago. I saw her about the same time she saw me and that's how we figured out who the two of us were, but we never talked about it. I just never felt any compulsion to tell anybody, primarily because I don't trust anybody. The longer I'm there, the people you think you can trust, for various and sundry reasons, just are not. There's nobody on the faculty that I'd confide anything to other than just general anger and frustration, faculty lounge chitchat. You never know. My former friend, who was also a teacher, told two people in his group and my first response was, "My God, what have you done? What's to keep people from talking?" He said, "Friendship." I said, "Friendship doesn't count squat when you're trying to work." But he doesn't think that will happen. His family was very supportive of the two of us. His mom was a delightful person. She supported him in everything he's done. His dad was extremely supportive of me as a person. He told these people. I told him, "I think you're crazy," because, again you don't know what people are going to do, even your own family. So I don't trust anybody. I know that when push comes to shove, well, I even chose another physician because the one I wanted, his wife works at my school. I know how people are. Boom, a matter of moments and it's blown away. That's why I've always lived on this side of town and taught on the other side of town. So that if I have a relationship there is no one to see us coming and going, or in the grocery store.

The new club that opened up here, I haven't been to it yet because it's on a street and across the street from it is a house. I don't know who the hell lives in that house and I work very near there. Everyone says you can pull in the back of the club and go in the back door. It's like, no way. I remember a friend who was driving to a bar one night and saw three girls walking across the street near that club. The girls were his students and he panicked. The girls told me this! It's easier to just not go out because of where the place is. I certainly don't need to run into someone there. I've become somewhat of a hermit, actually. And I'm not terribly disappointed. There are times, there are times, but all in all I find the longer I'm by myself the easier it is to deal with it. If you had told me this a couple of years ago, I'd probably have told you you were crazy because I was one of those that if I wasn't with somebody, I was out Friday and Saturday nights. After my five-year relationship broke up, I was out and about and not having a whole lot of fun doing it. That stopped me from getting depressed and going out on Saturday nights.

I once read a book about keeping a journal of my life, so I have a couple of spiral notebooks. I was telling a couple of people at work, it's amazing how sane my life is. It's just easier sometimes to be by yourself. It's just easier. I'm not running into people. And from a religious perspective, it's a great deal easier on me. And when you do certain things, you don't have to worry about getting to the confessional. Luckily for me, honest to God, I must confess this to anyone who will listen to me, that I have been lucky as hell in the priests that I know whether they be gay priests or they be just priests—gay, straight, whatever. With one exception, no one has ever treated me any less than just a decent guy, which is exactly, you know, what I am. I remember once in college, it was right after my summer soirée here, my first real event I ever experienced, after mass one morning. I confessed, and the priest wasn't judgmental. He wasn't judgmental. That same kind of thing, I guess, as when I was with my partner. It was the best it's ever been, the best it will ever be.

I stopped going to church, stopped going to Communion when my partner and I were together. That's something else. In the last year since I've been by myself, I find church very reassuring. I sat while everyone else was going to Communion. And I must tell you that I wonder if all those people are in a state of grace or are going to hell. It seems nobody goes to confession but the Communion rounds are filled.

I had a brief soirée last summer. Oh, a lovely man, but he was far too effeminate. Anyway, it was like a contest between my heart and my genitals. My genitals found him extremely appealing. My heart said, "No, you're much happier with yourself if you put your sex drive aside." Then Saturday night rolls around and I'm gonna sit in church on the bench.

God was smiling on me again. Here's this old guy whose wife died and he became a priest. It was funny, this was Christmas before last, I went out for one of those pre–Christmas confessions, and the lines were six or eight people long. I was surprised because usually I walk in and I'm the only person there. But pleasantly surprised, you understand. But anyhow, I stood in line and a person was inside. I stayed in this guy's line and waited. He's the sweetest, kindest man I've ever met. I told him things I'm not sure I would have told anyone else.

There was another priest in this city who will not admit to himself what he is, but he latches onto gay people. Talk about another betrayal. I told him things in confidence—though not in the confessional—and he made some comment to a friend who was upset enough to call me and tell me what happened. This infuriated me! He had betrayed my partner once, who wouldn't let him back in our house. Then this situation. I called and left a message on his machine, "How dare you do this?" I'm sort of a pre-Trent, post-Vatican II Catholic. I know I ramble, I do it quite often, but it's that trust of people. You think you can trust people then something happens. It's a very cruel thing for you.

Luckily for me, I never got in trouble. I remember a long time ago when the tubs (the Jacksonville City Bath Club) first opened—oh, I go back pretty far in this area—over 20 years ago, the local authorities didn't know what the place was. They thought it was a gambling joint, busted it, and took all the records. Well, for about a good week this town was in a total panic about the release of membership names. Once it became evident what it was—I'm not sure if it made it better or worse—I don't know. But anyhow, I remember sitting at Brothers (Night Club) for several nights in a row, on nights when I'd have to go to work the next day, waiting for the first edition of the paper to see if the names had been published. It turned out there were pretty prominent people's names on the list. It all finally blew over, but people remember. That was as close as I've ever come to having something revealed that I didn't want revealed. I've just found it easier not to tell people who aren't already members of the community, if you will.

Ronni: What do you think would happen if your principal found out?

Len: I don't know. I don't suppose he could fire me without detailed descriptive videotaped evidence maybe. Something of that nature. They used to have witch hunts in this county many years ago. I remember the first time I went to the bar. I wouldn't go in there for the longest time because I heard security was in there looking for teachers. The principal I have now I would trust as far as I could throw her. The one I had for the longest time of continuous service in school, I would have said to you that he would say, "As long as you're doing a good job, until you do something that could compromise your position here, I really don't care," though I'm speaking only from conjecture and not from reality. This one, well, it depends on great sum of the principal. There is one principal in the county who is notorious. I know one person who quit teaching, not because the principal was anti–gay, but just the opposite—because he was gay. The principal went after the teacher—sexual harassment. The teacher said to the principal, "Leave me the hell alone." When he said that to the principal, the principal made his life a living hell and he quit teaching, which was too bad because he might still be in the profession. He certainly was a very good teacher. I know of two other gay principals. Both of them have been around as long as I have.

You know, we have annual evaluations. Last year was the first time in 24 years I received even the slightest negative comment on my form. This year it's all brilliant. Last year my principal came to my class to visit and said something critical. This year there wasn't even a visit. I don't understand, but it was a very nice evaluation. So I don't know what he would say if he knew. I know there are some people on the faculty who would be very upset, not because they like me, but because they hate queers. We've got a couple of fellows who are real rabidly religious fanatical fruitcakes. I mean, these people are rabid. It's like (Jerry) Falwell's on the warpath again and these are the kind of people who would follow Falwell. Others might say, "Gee, I knew that years ago. What's the big deal? He does his job."

Something that's been detrimental to my mental health is I don't think I'm as good a teacher as I was. I can't figure out what the hell is the reason. Well, one reason, I think, is when you're by yourself as much as I am, you have no one to come home and beat up on. In that sense you tend to beat up on the kids more than you should. I would say that I've probably been nastier than I've been in a couple of other years, but that's something I take credit for. I've charmed some very important parents in this town, lots of politicians' kids, doctors' kids, lawyers' kids, indian chiefs' kids, and to the best of my recollection, 90% of those people felt like I did a pretty good job with those kids.

Ronni: What does it feel like when you hear derogatory words from colleagues?

Len: Well, there was an incident with this girl in my class whose sister I taught several years earlier had a baby. Someone asked what the baby's name was. When the student told him, someone else in the room said, "That sounds like a faggot name." Well, I tried to explain what a faggot is, first of all, and I tried to do it in a way so as not to open up too many doors of inquiry. I told them that in the Middle Ages for crimes punishable by death, a bundle of wood—called a *faggot*—was placed around the foot of the person to be burned at the stake. The crowd would scream, "Burn, faggot, burn." I didn't know if that made a difference of not. And, yeah, I'm guilty of it, too. One of our sweet, wonderful kids was showing his prom pictures around and I said, "Sissy." I knew I shouldn't have done it. It was innocent. To be perfectly blunt, it doesn't bother me all that much. Maybe if they said it to me in a hurtful way and they said it in a vicious way, and I was worried about what they might do to me, but I've never been a champion, not out there on the front lines, as you are. I love you and I'm glad there are people like you out there. I'm not a crusader. I understand what the straight community feels about us. Yes, to a certain extent, education will change those attitudes, but to a greater extent nothing you can tell them will change their attitudes about what they believe to be a perversion somewhere. I mean, when you stop to think about it—gay sex versus straight sex—it's kind of frightening in a lot of ways. While we're *not* sex, we're people, sex is what people, you know, well, what makes us different is the sex that we have. I mean, if you stop to think about it, sometimes maybe men and women do these things with each other too, but not as regularly. And as such, it's easy to understand their nervousness about it. I'm always very leery of people who claim to be accepting of us because I don't think they really know what they're accepting per se. Do they stop and think about what we do down the hall? No, it's none of their business, number one, but are they being politically correct, which is the latest term? Are they accepting you as you are, and so on and so forth? Is it some kind of misguided compassion?

I work with people, but I never socialize with people from work strictly, because I have nothing in common with them other than the workplace. So when I go home in the afternoon, the last thing I want to do is socialize with the teachers because all we do is bitch about the kids. So I don't have social relationships with them.

You know, I hate the word *lover*. I despise that word. Sounds so clan-destine. Anyhow, in that regard, I understand how people feel. Maybe because I grew up being told it was so corrupt, so bad, but then, I grew up hearing that sex was bad. Sex was something you had in marriage, period. In reading and watching and listening, I haven't found that atti-tude is basically changed. I don't think there's the condemnation of peo-ple there once was. Honest to God, I don't want the church to change its mind. I don't want the church to come out and say just because we're in the '90s, the age of political correctness, that 2,000 years of teaching is out the window. I don't think that 2,000 years of tradition of male priest-hood should, because of popular opinion, be changed into allowing women to be ordained priests. Again, I don't have a problem with things the way they are because I understand.

I would love to be able to invite my friend here and say, "Mom and Dad, this is so-and-so who I love more than life itself." But that won't happen. I understand that people don't seem to want to know. It's like, if you don't get in my face, I won't get in yours. If you get in my face I'm going to get angry with you. Again, maybe I go back to my religious roots which may be a cop-out, but I don't think this is what I was taught. This is what I accepted as truth, I still accept it as truth. I deviate from the truth sometimes and when I do, I separate myself from the church in certain ways. And I don't say this out of any sense of self-righteous im-portance. I don't miss mass. To not go without a valid good reason would be a grievous matter. The church said it's a grievous matter.

The sex was something that I had a really difficult time dealing with. As long as my partner and I were together, we quit going to church. That bothered me, but what really bothered me was that in the eyes of the church I was doing something wrong. And I cannot sit here and tell you that the church doesn't know what the hell it's talking about. Because if I said that, I'd have to ask what in the hell am I doing here in the first place. This church that I belong to, that I was raised in, that I believe wholeheartedly, and that I intend to be buried in, is right on this issue. I am simply in conflict with my church. Because I am in conflict with my church doesn't mean my church has turned away from me. It offers me opportunity to undo the conflict. Again, I'm not one who's going to say, "If it's love, God won't mind." He does mind. He minds about a lot of things that we do and don't do. He creates. We try so hard to create an image of ourselves that is acceptable, but there are rules and regulations that we're never going to be able to fit ourselves into. I don't believe in discrimination of any sort. Neither do I believe in any of the legislative things to protect people based on sexual orientation. I just don't believe that.

Ronni: When you are teaching your class and you teach about Margaret Mead, for example, do you include the fact that she was a lesbian?

Len: Of course! Oh, yeah! Well, let me put it to you this way. We just finished the Enlightenment several weeks ago. Voltaire and Frederick the Great were gay men. I told the class that. I heard one voice say, "How do you know?" My response was, "Well, I read." And, of course, James I, after whom the Bible was named. Mary Stewart's husband, I tell them about him and why they did what they did to him was because of what he was. He was blown up because he was having an affair quite openly with some man. And they asked, "Well, how did he have a baby by her?" I told them that a lot of men did their dynastic duties, but they had much more fun doing other things. You've got to be very careful here because you don't want them going home and saying, "My teacher was saying da-da-da-da-da." By the same token, I want them to know. I don't know how many other people tell them these stories or not. I know, so subjects like James I being gay or Mary Stewart's husband being gay would probably not enter into their teaching. I mention it, but I do it in such a way to get the information across without being revelatory about myself.

Ronni: You're providing role models for these kids. You're saying to the lesbian or gay young person in your classroom that they're not alone, not the only one, that there are heroes and famous people who felt just like they feel.

Len: To be perfectly frank with you, I never thought about that and if that's the case, so be it. It's not intentional on my part. I don't look at the kids like, well, the kids you figure out are those who look either sissy or real butch. In fact, I know I have a girl in class who is. Apparently she comes from an excruciatingly poor home. I worry about her sometimes that older people, male and female, sometimes find these kids, find them vulnerable and take advantage of their vulnerabilities. It's something I've never done. Sure, you feel like reaching out, but you don't for your own safety's sake. But, yeah, if this kid learns there are others out there, but that's not a conscious thing on my part. I was introducing the subject to them to show them that there are great characters that are gay and have made lasting contributions to humanity. But I don't start off from that premise. I don't want you to think that even in a subtle way that I'm teaching gay history. I am not. That's not my point. My point is to teach them that there are people out there, Michelangelo, David. Sometimes I wonder if we don't invent our own heroes. We *want* them to be heroes.

I said to myself the other day, I finally figured out why blacks call each other *niggers*. It's the same as we in our community calling each other derogatory terms. As long as no one else is calling us that, it doesn't have the same meaning. If you call someone a *faggot* in a joking way it's taken as a joke, but if someone else calls you a *faggot* in a non-joking way, you take offense. Well, it's the same thing with blacks using the word *nigger*. I hate it when I hear the kids do it and I'll correct them if I have the opportunity, but realized two weeks ago that a minority is a minority is a minority. The only way for minorities to get respect is to stop considering themselves minorities. Don't call yourself *nigger* if you're black, or in feminine terms if you're a man. Maybe then you'll stop hating yourself. We all hate ourselves in some way. We do. We'd all like to be out there. We'd all like to be normal with all that normalcy brings with it. We can't. We won't. I've never been a disciple of people who can change. We can't. God knows, if anybody would have been in that therapy it would have been me if it works, but it doesn't. Going out is too damned depressing. I don't think that the straight world is as youth-conscious as it once was, but I remember when I turned 30, I read in a magazine in a doctor's office that 30 years of age was considered old age in the gay world. I sat in my womb chair and cried my eyes out. I'll be 47 in July and I look forward to it. Forty-seven sounds old for some reason. This one bothers me. The youth culture, being around young people as I am all day, yet I feel more distant from them than I used to.

This is the dichotomy of me. In so many ways, I'm an arch-conservative. Pious XII was the last real Catholic pope as far as I'm concerned, but anyhow, in many areas I'm an absolute conservative. In other areas, I'm a flagrant liberal in the sense of what-the-hell difference does it make what the kids wear to school as long as they show up. Kids have been defying authority since time immemorial. It's not going to change now because Jerry Falwell or Pat Robertson comes out and says da-da-da-da-da-da. Kids are only teenagers for a short while and then it's over. Listening to me talk for all this time, you can obviously tell I have conservative ideas on many things but I'm a flaming liberal on others.

I think I've finally run out of things to say and I'm pooped. I feel like I've bared my soul to this woman I don't even know.

Be gentle. . . . (laughter and a hug).

Len did not live to celebrate his 48th birthday. He is remembered here with gratitude.

ELISA

I met Elisa at her house after school one afternoon. A native of northeast Florida, she is a small, colorful, vibrant woman in her early 30s. She was a high school teacher who lived with her partner of five years. They owned their home and socialized primarily with other lesbians. I called

Elisa and asked if I might interview her because she lived the experience of every teacher's nightmare: She was accused of molesting a female student.

Ronni: When did you come out?

Elisa: Right at the end of my senior year in high school. In fact, I was pretty lucky because I'm probably one of the very few in our community who came out before I had any type of sexual experience, and I was out for five years before I got into a relationship. So I think I'm kind of unique. I did it in my mind before I actually did it. I think most people put the cart before the horse.

Ronni: You went into teaching knowing you were a lesbian?

Elisa: Yes. And I didn't think about it being risky. In fact, I went into it the other way. I went into it—and this was probably stupid—but I was thinking, "Wouldn't it be nice for gay and lesbian teenagers to have some role models to look up to?" But of course now, especially after what I went through, that can't happen, especially in this area. In other areas it may be possible, but not here.

Ronni: Please talk about your experience.

Elisa: Wow . . . I hope you have a long tape. Well, a student—this was last school year—came out to me, and it's not only that she came out to me, but she also was here at my house because she was having big problems at home. She was from Richmond and came here to live with a relative. Her relative wasn't around and she ended up by herself in a bad gang area. Actually, before she came out to me I realized she was kind of alone, and I thought, "Ha! I can save the world," and wouldn't it be nice. Once while she was staying at her relative's house, she told me the phone was out. She'd just gotten out of the hospital and her relative was at the beach. What are you supposed to do? So, stupid me, with her relative's permission, which I found out now doesn't mean anything, I brought her to stay at my house on the couch in the back. Eventually she came out to me and I thought everything was fine. She talked about her problems and, you know, older sister kind of thing. I thought everything was just fine. With the attention, she seemed to be doing much better in school.

She seemed to improve when—viola! Suddenly she had to move and suddenly she was leaving and why was she leaving? She didn't want to, but she said she had to. I was at a total loss. She backed away from me, didn't talk to me as much, didn't come to see me as much, didn't do this, this, and this. Then one night I came home from a basketball game at school. This was right before she was supposed to leave to go back to Richmond. When I got home, someone's car was in my driveway. It was the student's relative, which was really weird, and the student was there, too. She was there to confront my partner and me. The student claimed that she was—oh, I don't remember what the word was they used—sexually molested, assaulted, I don't know. She accused both my partner and me. Then the story changed the next day to just my partner.

That happened in January. By the end of February, my partner had actually been arrested. The whole reason the aunt or whoever she was was here was for money. She said that if we didn't give her money they would go to the school board. Apparently they thought if they didn't get money from us, the school board would give them money to keep it quiet.

Ronni: When did you first bring the girl home with you?

Elisa: October. Then this happened in January, these allegations came out. Then my partner was arrested. That night we called everybody we knew. A friend who's an attorney went with me to talk to my principal. I told my principal what happened. I went to the (teachers') union. I was really amazed by all this. I had to go to the union rep (representative) at my school, who is gay. I went to one of the lawyers at the union, who is also gay. Even though it was very traumatic, I was very lucky. Can you imagine if I had to go to the union lawyer and say, "I'm a lesbian"? So I was real lucky with that. But my partner ended up getting arrested. Everyone said, "Well, it won't go any further because they don't have any proof." But every time people said that it wasn't going to go on, it went on. And on and on and on. It was the craziest thing! I mean, my partner was arrested! We had to waste $1,000 on bail. Both she and I had to take lie detector tests. She had to pay for a lawyer and I had to pay for a lawyer because the union lawyer could only take it so far. We're now thousands of dollars in debt because of this.

You know how they have the speedy trial clock of six months? Well, my partner was arrested but never officially charged and we thought the speedy trial clock had started, so we were just waiting for the six months to pass. Her lawyer decided the best idea was not to piss off the prosecutor because apparently the prosecutor was crazy. He's just crazy. She would basically not contact him in hopes that it would be forgotten. Whatever. Well, every month someone in the student's family must have called because it would come up again. When it got to the six months, the lawyer called the prosecutor's office and said the six months are up. He said, "No, the six months doesn't start until she's been arraigned and she hasn't been arraigned yet." So for six months or longer, every Friday my partner thought she had to go to court, and every Thursday her lawyer would call and say, "No, you don't have to go." Finally, after that six months was up, my partner's lawyer was just going to wait a month more, but said to the prosecutor, "I'm going to bring you up on charges because this is harassment. You're not doing anything." Miraculously, three weeks after that, the charges were dropped and the case was let go. There were no charges officially brought against her. It was just over. And we have no idea why.

We had no idea what happened. And we can never find out. I don't know where the student is. I don't know what's happened to her. After this happened, she was supposedly put into a psycho ward somewhere. It was the most horrible thing.

I don't even know if she really was a lesbian. She was a 17-year-old student. I never saw her in a sexual act, not that that defines a lesbian, but when she got here she told me she had been in a relationship with a woman for x years in Richmond. From what I understand, that was part of the reason for sending her down to Florida.

Ronni: How does this change the way you might interact with students?

Elisa: I'm never alone with them. That's the main difference. I just will never be alone with a student. And I realize I made a big mistake, but I thought I could take care of it. I thought I was helping this young woman. That was a big mistake. That was me knowing that I'm a good person and thinking that everyone in the world is a good person. I was 27 years old. You know the novel of initiation you read in high school? I was 27 when I had to go through my initiation—my "Oh, Jeez, I guess the world isn't going to welcome me with open arms" aha. It was horrible. It took almost a year to get through all of it, from beginning to end. I remember my partner saying we could have had a baby in that time.

It was also a horrific thing just to think that someone who did not know me—these police officers, these prosecutors—were making judgments on me, and they had no idea. But I know it was because we're lesbians. I went to be interviewed on my partner's behalf by a detective from the sex crimes unit—I remember thinking the detective's name would be a great name for some kind of television show. Anyway, he was openly shocked at what I looked like, I could tell. I don't know if he thought that because I'm a lesbian I'd have grease on my face and blue jeans and a wrench in my pocket or what. I thought, "Oh, you poor man. You must be so closed off from reality."

I really learned. I think it's such a shame because you hear teachers talk or you see students who you know are gay, and you know who they are and what they're going through, and you think all they would need to know is that it's not so hard. And I can't do anything.

Ronni: What were you like before all this happened? How were you with the students?

Elisa: I think I'm not that much different now. At first when this happened, I just lost it. But now I think I'm almost back to the same. I'm not as physical. I'm a very physical person and I'm not as physical as I was with them. And I don't talk about my personal life.

Ronni: Do your students know you're a lesbian?

Elisa: No, I don't think so. When this happened, I think rumors went around. There were definitely rumors. Someone—bless their hearts, they couldn't even spell it right—put on my doorframe "D-I-K-E." I thought, "Oh, someone must have seen that I'm retaining water." You know? What can you do? And a rock got thrown through my window. I think that was because of it, so I just covered the hole with a target. I think that was over a two-week period of time. And a student told my best friend, another teacher at school. But it quieted down real quick. With teenagers, you know, their attention goes off in other directions. I think people bought into the rumor that I'm a lesbian for a time, but I don't fit their mold of looking like what a lesbian looks like so I think they don't really think it.

Ronni: Are there other lesbians in your school?

Elisa: No. There's a gay man in my school, but no lesbians that I know of.

Ronni: How about students?

Elisa: There are at least two gay males that I know of, students who are open basically. One I saw one night at the Club (gay bar)—and that's a cramp in the big ol' style. People say there are more gays and lesbians coming out of my high school, but I don't know. My school is more of a minority school and the black kids don't seem to be able to come out as well. I don't know. I don't know how to put that.

Ronni: Do you ever hear people using derogatory terms for lesbians and gays at school?

Elisa: Yes. Lots of times.

Ronni: Does anybody stop them? What do people do?

Elisa: Well, I try to stop it. I try to do it with humor. My discipline is with humor. I usually say, "If you agree with that, why don't you go out and get it over with?" That's normally what I say. Or if a guy says, "Oh, that guy's a *faggot*," I usually say, "I think it's interesting when guys think about other guys being *fags*." Well, I say it's *gay*, not *fags*, but I normally do it with humor. Because of what I teach, I try to get them used to proper vocabulary. I might say, "Who wears a dress?" They might say, "Women," but someone might say, "Well, guys could." And I'd say, "Yes, yes, and we're certainly not going to judge. And if that's what you want to do, gentlemen, that's fine." You know, so I try to jokingly bring in the fact that only women wear dresses isn't always true. But I do it with humor. Again, I can get away with it because no one will look at me and think I'm gay.

Ronni: Do you ever hear teachers using derogatory terms?

Elisa: Yes. *That* is the most offensive thing. That is the most offensive thing to me because I believe that educators are there to teach open-mindedness. We're not there to force our opinions on them. And we have a lot of teachers at our school who are holier than thou. They have all the answers to all the world's problems. We had a student, a male, who had two pierced ears. His teacher said, "I told him he shouldn't be wearing that." I said, "Oh, really? Why don't you spend that time trying to help him with his homework instead of criticizing him? That's what you're there for, not to tell him how to dress. They're not your ears and he's not your child." You know, we have a very old faculty. The next youngest person to me on the staff was like 15 years older than me. So they need a big ol' breath of fresh air.

Ronni: How are you with your principal now? You said you had to tell your principal about the problems you had with that female student.

Elisa: Well, actually, that was another problem. I felt like, well, I realized when I went through this, how the administration is on a totally separate level than teachers. They go into cover-your-ass mode real fast. When it was over, I remember thinking, "Gee, he's not very thrilled." But that's another story altogether. I don't deal with him unless I have to. He's very close to retirement and doesn't invest a lot of energy into many things anyway. It's tough.

Ronni: When there are school functions, do you take your partner with you?

Elisa: I did before this happened. I no longer will submit her to that.

Ronni: Do you feel you're more closeted now?

Elisa: Yes. As a matter of fact, in my life, period. I'm in a different mode than before. I have more friends who we do quiet things with. I'm not a "go-out-and-do-this-or-that" kind of person. But when this happened, for a while my partner and I wouldn't even be seen in public together. That's what the lawyer suggested, just in case the news did get hold of it. So for a while we wouldn't even ride in the same car. That was short-lived, maybe a month at the most. We're real careful here. We go out of town a lot, so we don't have to be so vigilant. Before that, I mean, my partner is so far out it's not even funny. She's had her picture in the newspaper, you know. So that was just a real slap for both of us and it stung real bad. So we go out of town a lot. When we go to bars locally, which isn't very often, we go in a large group. Since I once ran into a student there, I tend to go places where it's 21 and older as opposed to 18 and older, which some of the clubs are sometimes.

I don't know, I can't keep up with it all. But we're just not much for going out. We'll probably go to the Jacksonville Gay Pride event this year. I'll give it a try. I think I'm more worried for my partner's sake than for my own. In fact, I've been working on my resume and sending it out to places because I am almost to the point where I want to leave teaching. I want a job where I can have a rainbow sticker on my car. I hate not being able to be truthful with everyone. It gets too difficult to figure out who you've told what, when, and how, and I don't want to have to mess with it. I'm out now, except at school. I'm out to everyone I know. My family, it's done with, sometimes it's difficult to be one way here and another way there. It's tough.

Ronni: What do you think about the school board's reactions to gay people?

Elisa: I know they could fire me if they decided, but then I think that's fine. I'll just be the person who has to fight it. It's not the best for everybody, but it's going to have to be done eventually. This town is too backwards. This town is too run by the Baptist Church, and eventually someone's going to have to do something. Once on Channel 1—get this—there was an entire week devoted to AIDS. It started, but the minute the administration realized what was on, they ripped it off and we didn't get it. And remember when Miss America spoke in Jacksonville a few years ago? Her issue was AIDS and she was speaking all over the country to teenagers about it. But when she got to Jacksonville she was told she could talk about AIDS but couldn't mention the word *condom*! Imagine! We had dinner with a health department employee who does HIV counseling. She said lots of heterosexually active teens have HIV. I tell my kids this stuff, but I know I'm not supposed to. It's really stupid, and dangerous, not to mention it. I go the extra mile to tell my kids stuff when I know I'm not supposed to.

Ronni: Do you ever talk with them about sexual orientation?

Elisa: Not in a serious manner. Not really.

Ronni: I'm wondering about when you look out in your classroom and you know there are lesbian and gay kids out there, what goes through your mind?

Elisa: To be a good role model in my quiet way. Boy, that sounds weird! How can you be a role model and be quiet? But if you're not quiet, you're fired!

Ronni: Do you know about JASMYN?

Elisa: Yes. It would be a major problem for teachers to let their kids know about JASMYN or pass out flyers about them. In our school, where I think our guidance counselors are just a joke, if a student was really struggling with his or her sexuality, they could not go to their parents. If they went to the guidance counselor here, they'd get the same thing they got from their parents: "You just need to pray." I mean, literally. I don't know how our school is getting away with it. They're doing some crazy religious stuff. I wouldn't send a kid to the counselor. In fact, I knew a girl who went to the guidance counselor who told her it's just a phase. "You'll be fine. Go to church." That was the answer. I think it's really important to do something. There are too many, like someone said, kids kill themselves over the things we can't talk to them about. We can't talk about masturbation, about homosexuality. I mean, those are the big two. And AIDS and pregnancy. I've got girls left and right who are pregnant. It just makes me sick for these kids. It's very disconcerting. And these gay kids, the fact that they're aware says a lot about them, and they should be treated like adults when they're making decisions. I'm afraid that too many people in the school think they're just kids going through a phase. If a person is old enough to realize that there's something different about them, they're old enough to be dealt with as an individual and not through their parents. It's a drag.

Ronni: So, given all this stuff, what does it feel like to be a lesbian teacher in this county?

Elisa: It was fine until a year and a half ago. I'm at a point now where I'm looking for something comparable in the private sector. I'll get paid elsewhere. I know too many people in the private sector who can live their lives. I go to my partner's functions, literally every function at her office is open to spouses and significant others, just because of us. I'm the only significant other and that's the reason they chose that term. That makes me very jealous! That makes me want what I deserve. I don't deserve to go through what most, what all gay teachers have to do—to lie. I thought, oh, how sad. I don't want to live my life like that, thank you very much. It's ridiculous. Kids are taught the stuff. I deal with minorities at school. I'm amazed to see how closed-minded they are about the lesbian and gay communities. You know, "my minority is more important than your minority." Well, I don't think so.

It's just so important that someone do something in the public schools. That's where a majority of kids go. We're losing. Literally, physically, those kids are doing something to themselves. It's very scary.

Ronni: What do you think needs to happen to change the process?

Elisa: Education, but then with that comes so much of a problem. You've got to educate parents. You've got to teach the teachers. Some of the teachers just amaze me with their stupidity. Lighten up a little, please. I don't understand why they don't, well, I guess it's because they think they have all the answers. They go to their church and they pray to their God. They know what He wants, and that's not it. They know it. It's so scary. I wouldn't want to be the one to start fishing it out, though. I'll complain till they do something about it. It that good? I just wish, it would be great, if just one day all teachers, administrators, support personnel and staff would just come out. That would about do it. That would do a lot. There are a huge number of lesbian and gay people in the school system here. It's just amazing and it's scary! It's even scarier to think how closeted many of them are. Well, it's a shame that that's necessary. Again, after all I've been through this last year, it's just necessary. People live their lives in such paranoid fashion, petrified that anybody would find out. And it seems that the older people get and the more comfortable they get, the more scared and closeted they become. They'll lose it all. It's sad. Luckily, my partner and I have such a great network of friends. We have plenty to do. We just do it in a different fashion. But, I don't know, maybe it's just us being more grown-up, period. Going out all the time isn't so much fun anymore. It's such a problem. It would be so much easier if you couldn't hide, if we all had lavender skin and were easily identifiable. You think you're fine until you run into your students in the mall. They're everywhere. I hated living in the same neighborhood as the school. I like having more distance between me and the kids.

Ronni: How long have you been teaching in this county?

Elisa: Well, I substituted for two years and I've been teaching for three and a half. I'm up for tenure next year, but I don't know if I'll make it.

It's just such a problem. One of our teacher's daughters is a lesbian who I know separately from her parent. And the athletes. If nothing else, they should be aware of it, especially the female athletes who will go to college and get it full in the face. They have to know how to deal with it, how to get along with it. I had to learn how to deal with the fact that I'm white and have to deal with a lot of black people. You just have to learn to deal with the differences. They're there. You can't ignore them and pretend the differences aren't there because they are. You can't ignore them because if you're scared, the kids smell fear on you.

I fight having to be closeted. I want to be able to be open with my kids. But there aren't many choices. I don't know if it's better in other places. Maybe it is. Even in the most progressive cities, you still have the problems in education. Teachers are supposed to be role models.

I also don't think that kids should be placed in special schools because they're gay. They should learn to live with everyone else, just like everyone else needs to learn to live with gay people. I have a student whose parents kicked him out of the house. He's homeless. He lives with boyfriends. I don't know who he lives with. He barely keeps his car running so he can get back and forth to work and go to school. But he's gay, and so what, and he's accepted by his friends. He's a senior, and they accept him. He's way out. And he's black, too. It's tough for him. I know very few women of color who are out. I can't place my finger on it, but it seems to be more difficult for them.

We just have to keep fighting in this area because this place is so run by the conservative un-christian people. These people who think they know what's right and they can judge others. They're so un-christian in their opinions. My mother really didn't deal with my being a lesbian until this thing happened with the student. Then she had to come to grips with it. Her pastor was just wonderful. He said what's important was a healthy relationship. If the relationship is healthy, then how can anything be wrong?

Neither Elisa nor her partner were charged with any crimes, but Elisa was unable to continue teaching in what she described as the "repressive climate" of northeast Florida. Although Elisa was not personally known by the other participants in this study, all were aware of the charges she and her partner faced, and all talked about their continued—and now recently validated—sense of vulnerability.

SHERRY

Sherry and I met in her home one evening. She is a woman in her mid-40s, single, and shares her home with a woman who was once her partner. The housemate, who was not at home at the time of the interview, is also a teacher in the public school system. Sherry identifies herself as being politically active and felt she would be helping young lesbian and gay people by participating in this study. She was quite animated in sharing her story and adamant about telling it in chronological order. I found her to be informative, knowledgeable, and extremely entertaining.

Ronni: Please talk about what it's like to be a lesbian in the school system in northeast Florida.
Sherry: Wait. I want to give you the whole history. Do you want my gay history or my professional history?
Ronni: Both, especially as they intersect.
Sherry: Okay, we'll do personal history and you can hear the whole thing. In essence it all connects. I guess all little girls experiment, and I really enjoyed the experiments. When I was 12, I met another 12-year-old girl and we became friends for 10 years. We weren't lovers until we were about 16. But we didn't know what to do until that time. It was in the '60s after all. I mean, we experimented, but we really didn't know what to do. We finally figured it out. While we were in high school, I was president of Future Teachers of America and she was the vice-

president. I always knew I was going to teach. Anyway, everything I did, she did. After graduation from high school, we went our separate ways because we went to different colleges. We maintained a correspondence, but the sexual aspect of it was long gone.

I got married right after college. That was short-lived. I had an affair with a woman while I was married and remembered exactly what life was all about. I came to the northeast Florida area in the early '70s, after my divorce. I came down here for a wedding of a friend and stayed. I got a job teaching almost immediately.

Where sexuality and teaching come together starts now. My first assignment—can I mention school names?

Ronni: School names will not be used.

Sherry: Okay, if I mention them, please delete them later.

Ronni: I will.

Sherry: My first assignment was at [school name]. The kids there had records longer than my arm and your arm put together. These kids thought nothing of carrying guns to school and putting them on their desks in the classroom. I'd send someone to the office, the principal would come and pick up the gun, and that was that.

I didn't know about gay bars in northeast Florida then. I knew nothing. I didn't even think I wanted to have, you know, my normal sexual appetite satisfied. It wasn't worth it because the fear of the superintendent was in me. You couldn't even go to a straight bar. If you were seen coming out of a bar, you would lose your job because teachers weren't supposed to drink. And besides that, I needed my $7,000-a-year salary. That was in the late '70s.

I remember one afternoon after school—there were only two other women teachers on my wing—one woman came into my room. She said, "Come have a drink with me after school. I think I need to talk." Okay, fine, so we had a drink, we had a little chat, and she got me to join the (teachers') union. I thought nothing of it. Then one day a little later, she asked me if I could drive her home the next day. So I drive her home the next day, and here comes her partner and plants a big kiss on her. Now I'm not embarrassed or anything like that, so she says, "I thought so." I said, "For Christ sake, all you had to do was ask me." I was 25 years old. What the f--- do I know? You can edit that out, too. So what proceeded was an evening where we all got very drunk. I was very happy that there was somebody I could finally talk to.

Turned out I was wrong, not that I couldn't talk to her, but she was an alcoholic and I didn't need that. I mean, I was 25 and at 25 it was okay to get drunk, looking back. That's not the stuff that you do anymore. But nonetheless, that was when I met the legendary Mayport Mary and that whole crowd. Mayport Mary comes up to you and says, "Oh you're another one of them teachers." I was drinking Southern Comfort 'til morning, because when Mayport Mary tells you to drink in her bar, you drink in her bar—especially when she's buying! So then I got introduced to all the bars because that's where the special scenes were. The French Quarter (now-defunct gay bar in Jacksonville)—Bubbles was still alive—that was really a neat scene—a whole slew of teachers. But I wasn't really comfortable, because this was the seamy side of being a lesbian and these were professional women. They were in a butch-femme 1950s mindset that really didn't mix with who I was. Basically, I have a more feminist mindset and far more class than this. I think that's exactly how to put it.

I didn't like the Little Dude (lesbian bar in Jacksonville) then either, although lots of teachers went there, too. I was uncomfortable there, too, because this was not my scene. I got involved with the Pagoda (a lesbian-feminist commune in Vilano Beach near St. Augustine). Through the Pagoda and through a woman I was seeing, I met more feminist teachers who were of my own ilk. I also met several key people in the community. I met a different class of lesbians. And I met lesbian administrators in northeast Florida schools, too, at the bars. While I'm not invited to their parties, I know who they all are. There's a big class difference in the lesbian community here in the school districts. There are principals and the people at the county offices that are lesbians. They don't associate with us regular teachers. Occasionally you'll see one of them at the bars, but not often.

I was transferred to a school where the principal was a lesbian. I knew her, she knew me, and basically we knew each other's score. And that would have been fine, except that she began to have an affair with another female teacher who was off the same period I was, another lesbian who I knew. I didn't like it. I mean, I really didn't care who she was sleeping with—that didn't bother me at all. But what did bother me a lot was that she would go into her office, lock the door, and you and I both know what was going on. They would play little footsie games under the table at lunch, which embarrassed me to death. I went to her and said, "Get me outta here, 'cause if you don't . . . ." I mean, everyone, her secretary, everyone knew what was going on. It was so bad for lesbians in general. Her secretary was the wife of a school board member, okay? What a mess! I mean, you don't do this shit, but no one said anything.
Ronni: But people knew?
Sherry: How could you *not* know? They came to school together. Yes, people knew. It was embarrassing. Be a little more discrete, please!

Other things. I met what's-her-face whose name I will not mention. We didn't teach together at first, but we did teach together (in the same school) later. Big mistake! I met my next partner through union activity. The president of the union knew very well that I was a lesbian. I came out to her. Her philosophy was, if you can help me, I'll take your help. Interestingly, a lot of union people in Florida are gay. I'll leave it at that. I don't want to out anybody. If you turn that off I'll . . . .

Ronni: That's okay. I don't want you to out anybody.

Sherry: Okay. So, but I'm saying, a lot of union staff statewide are gay. It's an easy profession. So, where was I in my chronology? Oh, I'm in the middle of the '80s now. So I met people. At that school there were a lot more gay people, lot more gay teachers that I met. I met some gay counselors, too.

Oh, I didn't finish my story about the French Quarter. I need to go back to that. We were sitting there, about six teachers sitting at the table, all from various schools. Mysteriously, Bubbles brings a whole trayfull of drinks to our table that we didn't order, and Bubbles says, "Over there bought you these drinks." So we turned around, and it was a table full of our students! You know, I took off the next three days! I was afraid to show my face, and they called up laughing at me. I was terrified! Now, basically, if you see me there and you say something, what were *you* doing there? That's my attitude now. But then, I mean, we're talking 15 years ago. It was rough. So, after my partner and I got together we went to a couple of bars. We go into Brothers one winter evening, and one of her students took her coat. Oh, she was so embarrassed! That soured her. She won't go out now unless under extreme coercion.

Ronni: I remember one time at Brothers, I was with a teacher who had students, current students, of hers come into the bar. She literally crawled on the floor of the bar to the bathroom to avoid being seen by them!

Sherry: Oh, yeah. I've seen students in Brothers and I've seen students in a lot of places. When I started at [school], the gay kids gravitated toward me. Now it's different. The kids walk down the hall saying *dyke*. They somehow must have figured out I'm gay. At first it bothered me, then after a while I said, "Phfftt." You know, I don't care. You give in to them, then they know they're right. But you don't want to give in, so why do you? Because you sign a paper in the state of Florida, an ethics paper, that says what you can and what you can't do. Basically, you sign that paper or you don't work.

Ronni: It lists specific behaviors?

Sherry: No. No. It more or less talks about moral turpitude (Florida Statutes, 1995c), about conducting yourself in an upstanding and biblical way, you know. It doesn't say biblical per se, but you understand what they're talking about. You have to sign it—state requirement. The county requires it, too. You sign this ethics thing. Anyway, along about this time, I was out to a few people at school. I've always had the attitude that I care, but I don't care. I have to trust. I've trusted some people and that's been okay. Now I don't trust as many people, for reasons that I'll tell you later on.

At the time, 1984 to '85, I had a student fall in love with me. You know, that's really the hardest thing in the world to deal with. I remember having a very large crush on a teacher when I was in high school. She never knew that I was in love with her. Anyway, this young lady fell in love with me, and I would get a little gift. For three or four months I got anonymous stuff on my desk, you know how it is. And then, when she finally came to me and told me she was in love with me, I didn't know what to do. I had to come out to a few people, including the guidance counselor to deal with this.

Ronni: Wait a second. If this was anonymous, how did you know it was a girl?

Sherry: I wish I would have saved the stuff so you could see them. My class was really small, and I knew everybody's handwriting. I pretty much had an idea who it was. She finally came out to me, and she thought she was in love. She would call me on the phone. We would talk and I kept putting her off about going out. After she graduated, I still wouldn't go out with her. I had a partner. She finally said, "You'll never hear from me again." And I haven't. I knew she joined the air force and that's the last I heard from her. I'm sure she's living a gay old life somewhere. That was hard. In the meantime, I've had a lot of gay students come through my doors seeking safety.

Ronni: How would kids know to come to you?

Sherry: Well, you know, they don't really, but they drop little hints, mostly guys. I've only had two girls ever come to me. No, three. One killed herself. This one, another that came last year but wasn't in love with me, and the one who committed suicide. The one who committed suicide I didn't really know. I taught her sister. Her sister came to me and said, "You're a good person to talk to. I'll send my sister to talk to you." And I talked to her sister. This girl was going to kill herself anyway. There wasn't a whole lot I could do, but still I felt like I could have done something, but I really couldn't help her beyond the usual means of help.

Ronni: A female teacher I interviewed said that no female students ever came to talk to her, but male students did.

Sherry: Yes, and I'll tell you, I must have had three or four dozen gay male students. I still know them all, I still see them. In fact, one of them, a couple of them, are in the army. I correspond with them.

Ronni: What is it like when a student comes to you? What do they ask?

Sherry: We never talk about being gay. We never talk about that. But you can tell that the guy's gay. He mentions or drops a word or two and you pick up on it, but you don't say anything. One talked about the places he wanted to go. You kind of dance around those issues, but you know. Basically, like for example, one of my students I just saw at the In Touch (a gay bar in Jacksonville) last week. I knew he was gay and he knew I was gay and we just don't talk about it. So how does that hit you? I've taught a lot of kids over the years. They go by.

Ronni: So rather than talk about sexual orientation issues, it sounds like you talk about life issues?

Sherry: Yeah, I try to be a safe place for them where they can just come and talk. Yeah, talk, let some steam off, exactly. Because I'm not going to judge them. But I'm not going to say anything to them, because you can't. The guidance counselor, for example, who I talked to about the student, she said, "Well, you know, you can't say anything." I said, "I know." I asked, "Have you ever had this happen to you?" She said she had a girl come to her and she called the girl's parents. The girl, while she's a lesbian now, I think she's messed up because her parents sent her to a shrink to change her. So from my position, you cannot say anything to these kids. I mean, if I said to a kid to contact JASMYN, do you know what would happen to me? Goodbye, job. The principal and the vice-principal probably wouldn't do much of anything unless the parents raised a stink. If the parent raised a stink, they would have to reprimand me and start procedures, depending on what the parent would want, okay? It just depends on what the parent would want to do. Parents have all the power here.

Ronni: So if you had a JASMYN flyer sticking out of your purse. . . .

Sherry: Never! Never.

Ronni: You couldn't give it to a kid?

Sherry: No, no, no, no, no. What I say I can always deny. What's on paper I can't deny.

Ronni: What if a kid comes in and asks about AIDS?

Sherry: Nope, not allowed to say that either. Three words are verboten in northeast Florida. Well, actually, there's four: *homosexuality, masturbation, abortion,* and *AIDS*. You don't say those words. Where I teach, we're really talking about Bible thumpers. I mean, I've talked about abortion with the kids off the cuff in private conversations because so many of the girls are pregnant.

Wait. Let me back up. I forgot where I was in my chronology here. Oh, yeah. We changed principals and this guy can't stand me. If I say anything sexual, he'd find a way to get me fired. He'd put that on the news! The current principal I have, I don't know if he knows anything about me or not. Are there gay people at school? Absolutely. And someone is bisexual. My principal must know. I never said anything to him, but he must know. His fiancée knows, because she is at the same school as my housemate, and my housemate and I were partners at the time. She knew that. And he gets messages from a lesbian, from a partner of someone out at UNF (University of North Florida). It's all intertwined. The vice-principal knows, and we talk about gay people all the time.

There was a teacher not long ago at my school. We became friends. We would exercise-walk after school everyday, and she would come to my room almost everyday to ask questions because I was helping her with her beginning-teacher packet. One day she came to me and said, "I don't want to tell you this, but some people here said I shouldn't hang around with you because you're a lesbian." She said they said people will think she's queer, too, and she was scared to remain friends with me. And these are people I work with, people I thought I was friends with! At that point, I never spoke to her again. I just gave her stuff back to her and said, "Have a nice life." And that was it. She and her queeny husband moved to another county in Florida.

I'll tell you how far it goes. Last year, my principal said a parent called and said I was discussing lesbian and gay issues in class. Well, first of all, I never discuss lesbian and gay issues, except when kids call each other *faggots*. I stop that shit because I don't like it. I do it as much as I can, but nobody else seems to give a crap about it.

Three years ago, I had a girl who was going with another girl. I had both of them in class, different classes. She had real problems with her home life and she would talk to me about it. I said to her, "I can't say anything to you." She said, "I know. I know about you." I said, "I can't say anything to you, do you understand?" I tried to impress upon her that I couldn't do anything about it. I feel like I'm a happy, healthy person when I'm not in that school building. When I'm in that building, I can't be myself. I can't let any of myself come through.

A principal died of AIDS a while back. People made comment, some parents made comment, but basically the school system covered it up. A lot of teachers have passed away with AIDS, good friends of mine. They worked as long as they could. There are teachers who will tell you there aren't homosexuals in this school system, queers are *not* teaching your children. Ha! It's all fear. Teachers should be the most liberal of all and they're not. Rush Limbaugh fans are all over the place in my school.

Ronni: You knew you were a lesbian prior to becoming a teacher. Did you think being a lesbian presented a liability for you?

Sherry: In truth, I never thought about it. See, it never occurred to me—maybe I'm an anomaly—but it never occurred to me that being a lesbian should preclude me from doing anything until, of course, I showed up in the Deep South. Well, I don't know if this is the Deep South. I don't know what northeast Florida is. It's pretty crappy, but I'm still here. At the time when I could get out there weren't jobs available. It was a bad time for teaching. Now, when good teaching jobs are opened, I can't get out because I have too much time in. Retirement's not portable. I'm locked in here pretty much. That's pretty sad.

Ronni: How does your life at school differ from someone who is a heterosexual female teacher?

Sherry: I don't talk about what I did Friday night or with who. I went to a movie, period. It's difficult. It's like in the teachers' lounge, they talk about who they went out with and what they did. I can't do that. And too many of our teachers thump that Bible all the time. I just don't know how they get away with it.

Profanity, if you use profanity like *nigger* around here and it happens twice, you need to be thinking about your next job. I know teachers who've had their license suspended for three or four months and had to attend multicultural classes and all this other stuff.

Ronni: So what happens if a teacher uses the word *faggot*?

Sherry: Not much, I can tell you that! Not much. Touching is a bad thing. We're told very emphatically never to be alone in a room with a student of either sex. Teaching has been demeaned to such a point because you don't know what the student will do. Now if I were to go up to a female student and go like this (touches my lower arm in a gentle, reassuring fashion) to ask if she's okay, I can't do that. The student might construe it as sexual. Then life is over. The teacher will never win. And the school system will protect an administrator before they ever protect a teacher.

There are a lot of gay teachers in northeast Florida. We all don't know each other. Some of us know each other, but I don't know them all. I know some of them, but not all. The AFT (American Federation of Teachers) has a gay teachers' caucus, but we can't get it here. You can't even start one because then you'd have to officially come out. I might as well be saying 'bye to my career. It's like the military. It really is like the military. If they catch me doing something, they can do whatever they want and make life so miserable. I would not recommend any young lesbian or gay kid to go into teaching unless they really sincerely were willing to live away from the school and not be involved in the community where they teach, which I am not.

Ronni: How far away would that have to be?

Sherry: Well, across the water, across the bridge, in a different county. If you teach in Clay, live in Duval. If you teach in St. Johns, live in Baker. Don't live somewhere where you'll see your students after school.

And the church! Did you know that our county has school board members who are deacons in the First Baptist Church? And all the people who want promotions go to the First Baptist Church. I don't know where the superintendent goes but I assume if it's not the First Baptist Church, it's a Baptist church somewhere. Or now it could be the Episcopal Church with that new right-wing bishop they got. I've got nothing against any of them. I'm the last person to say you shall not pray as you please. But they sure make our lives miserable.

There are so many gay teachers here. Let me tell you something. Teaching is an easy profession. By and large, what do gay people like to do? Travel, have weekends free, do this, that, or the other. What profession affords you that while not paying you an exorbitant wage but a decent one? You're off in the summer, you get two weeks at Christmas. I mean, Thanksgiving, every holiday you get a three-day weekend. It's a good profession for that. You know, it's also a good profession because it allows you the ability to serve, to give. We give of ourselves in the classroom every single day.

Ronni: But don't you think that's true of most teachers, straight or gay? Isn't that why they're there?

Sherry: Some, sure, probably most. There are good kids out there, and there are good teachers. There are some bad ones, too.

Ronni: Have you experienced students suffering from discrimination at school?

Sherry: All the time, all the time. If a kid's a little off, he's a *fag*.

Ronni: A little off, how?

Sherry: Basically, this is males, because girls generally don't come out and say *dyke*. They really don't say that to each other. It's interesting. They don't even call boys *fag*. What they say is, "Oh, that's so gay." For example, I have a guy now who has very nice handwriting. What I would give for such handwriting! The kids laugh at him and say, "You write like a sissy. You queer? You a fag?" In the meantime, this kid may not be gay but it's discrimination based on a stereotype.

Ronni: What could a closeted gay or lesbian teacher do to help these lesbian and gay students?

Sherry: Well, we're all closeted and we all have them and we know they're gay. You can be nice to them. You can be supportive of them without being obvious, but you can let them know you're there. You can say anything to help keep their spirits up. We could be role models, but I'm not sure how we can do that without coming out and getting fired.

Some role model! You can let them know that they're going to survive if they can just get through this time.

Sherry is looking forward to her early retirement. She plans to return to school and begin another career in an occupation in which she believes she will have more freedom to be herself. She is currently dating a high-level female administrator in one of the northeast Florida school districts.

Chapter 5

Making Meaning of Their Words

Harbeck (1992a) suggested that research about lesbian and gay teachers must accomplish two things. First, it should serve to enlighten and inform non-gay people in education about the issues and lives of lesbian and gay educators. Second, it must empower lesbian and gay educators to eliminate the isolation and fear with which they currently live. A third desired effect arises in the context of this study: Research about gay and lesbian teachers may also be a vehicle for proposing recommendations for change based on the experiences and the voices of these educators. Such changes must focus not only on the public school setting, but also on teacher education and educational leadership programs in schools and colleges.

This chapter discusses the analysis and interpretation of the data from the participant interviews, with each of the following sections presenting a particular theme or concept relevant to them. At the end of each section, a summary describes the data that emerged from the stories and experiences shared by this small, self-selected population of lesbian and gay public school teachers in northeast Florida.

A theoretical screen provided a means to organize and examine key ideas as they appeared in the literature and were reported in the data. This screen served as a tool to sift and sort the data, and provided the starting point for the development of an interpretive model (Figure 1) to represent the life experiences of these gay and lesbian educators.

The research began with a more simplified conceptual representation of these ideas based upon the literature. Initial representation of key concepts from the literature did not take into account the full range of those to whom these participants assigned power over their lives or the intense

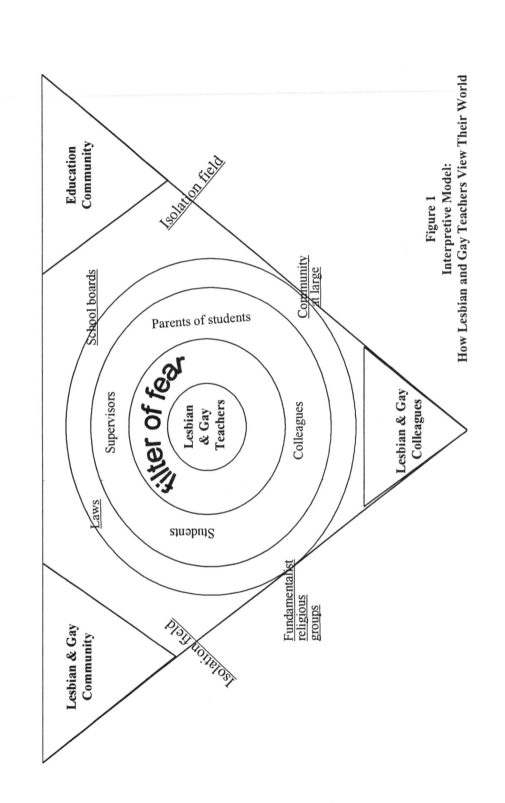

Figure 1
Interpretive Model:
How Lesbian and Gay Teachers View Their World

sense of isolation and pervasive fear of job loss articulated by the participants in this study.

The model depicts the lesbian or gay teacher at the center of the workplace, surrounded by a series of concentric circles. Between the teacher and the first layer of those with whom the teacher must interact is a filter of fear—of discovery, of harassment, and of job loss—through which the teacher views the world. Although the filter may not be activated 100% of the time for all the participants in this study, trigger events occur which cause the filter to activate and to become a barrier between the teacher and everyone else in the teacher's professional world.

Moving outward from the center, the first circle represents individuals with whom the teacher must professionally engage: students, parents of students, colleagues, supervisors, and administrators. The educators in this study believed that all the people in this first layer have power over them, especially in the area of job security. Between the teacher and the first layer of those with whom the teacher must interact is a filter of fear—of discovery, of harassment, and of job loss—through which the teacher views the world. Although the filter may not be activated 100% of the time for all the participants in this study, trigger events occur which cause the filter to activate and to become a barrier between the teacher and everyone else in the teacher's professional world.

The next outward concentric circle depicts those entities which determine the culture of the community as specifically named by the participants in this study: the community-at-large, the school boards, fundamentalist religious organizations, and Florida laws.

For some teachers in this study, the filter appears to be activated most of the time. Some events that may trigger filter activation include the following experiences: participants overhearing a colleague speak negatively of gay or lesbian people; a student calling another student a faggot; a media event involving lesbian or gay people; a school board discussion of forbidden terminology; election-year rhetoric; a party invitation to the principal's house; a celebration or vacation with a partner; illness or death of a partner. In the view of these participants, the list is virtually endless, and many of these situations are precarious; further, it is nearly impossible for these lesbian and gay teachers to ignore such trigger events.

The size of the concentric circles is fluid: The circles expand or contract depending on the experiences and perceptions of the teacher at the center. When events occur that are external to the participant, such as school board meetings or negative political discourse, there is an expansion of the circles, and feelings of intense isolation occur. When events occur that are personal and internal to the teacher, such as direct experiences of discrimination or observation of homophobic behaviors either in the work setting or when dealing with family issues, there is a feeling of constriction accompanying the sense of isolation.

The model contains one final component—a triangular design that supports the concentric circles that are found at its center. The triangle serves as a platform of isolation. In each apex of the triangle is a group from which the participants feel isolated: the large and diverse lesbian and gay community; lesbian and gay colleagues within the public school system; and the greater educational community.

Both the large military community of northeast Florida and the media are significant by their absence: None of the participants mentioned these entities as impacting the culture of northeast Florida, even though several of the participants are former military personnel. The issue here is not the accuracy of their perceptions, but rather the identification of people or organizations perceived by them to have great power.

The various elements in this model thus represent the perceptions of the participants in a visual form that may increase understanding of their experiences. The development of the model itself occurred as a tool to communicate the results of the analysis and interpretation of the data from the interviews. This model accounts for the full range of those to whom these participants assigned power over their lives. It also demonstrates the intense sense of isolation and pervasive fear of job loss articulated by the participants in this study. The remainder of this chapter discusses the analysis and interpretation of the data in terms of the key concepts and dynamics of experience identified by the participants themselves and represented in the model.

INTRODUCTION OF THE PARTICIPANTS

Great care was taken to avoid any possibility of identity discovery of the teachers who participated in this study. The people who shared their lives in this work did so at great personal risk and with tremendous trust in both the process and in me as researcher. They truly and vehemently believed they would lose their jobs as teachers if their identities were discovered, yet they were both willing and eager to tell their stories. In order to protect their identities, the names assigned to the participants are actually names of my own family members, all of whom live in California and Washington, and none of whom are in the teaching profession. The gender of the participants may also be reassigned in the narrative to add further protection from discovery attempts. Finally, their specific schools, districts, and grades are not revealed. Regardless of these changes, their stories are accurate. These teachers are the heroes of this work.

In addition to Barry, Elisa, Len, Barbra, and Sherry, whose stories you have already encountered, there are others. Barbara's partner, Lois, was also interviewed. Barbra and Lois met and fell in love when they became colleagues in the same school. Both women had been married to men previously. They still teach in the same school, although they believe nobody in the school knows about them. They drive separate cars to work and arrive from different directions so that suspicion is not aroused. Barbara used to host events in her home for several of the school's student groups. She quit doing that when she and Lois purchased a home together.

Sam retired from one of the branches of the armed forces about 25 years ago and has been a teacher ever since. His longtime partner died of an AIDS-related illness. Sam himself is HIV infected. He recently retired from teaching.

Katy and Ruth have been together for almost five years. Katy has been a teacher in the lower grades for 18 years, while Ruth is just embarking on her teaching career. Katy explained that she no longer hugs the younger students for fear of false accusations of inappropriate touching; she said she heard about another lesbian teacher who was accused of molesting an adolescent when she was simply being kind to the student. Both Katy and Ruth are deeply concerned about the cultural climate in northeast Florida and are considering moving to another state. Both are active in their religious community.

Carole, a teacher in northeast Florida for nearly eight years, was feeling down when we met. Earlier that day, she attended a party hosted by her school principal. Spouses and dates of colleagues were there, all apparently heterosexual. Carole would love to have had her partner of 11 years join her, but she felt that if she brought her, she would be admitting her lesbian identity and thus risking her job.

Sarah was a special education teacher in a public school in an upscale neighborhood. Since her interview for this project, she left Florida to teach elsewhere. She had been a teacher in northeast Florida for nearly 10 years. She said she didn't feel safe teaching and living in northeast Florida any longer, with the flagrant activities of the Christian Coalition and the Southern Baptist Church, especially when she observed them in her school. She expressed deep concern about lack of role models for lesbian and gay students, and felt that a number of students in her special education classes were dealing with their own sexual orientation issues.

Hal also left Florida and the teaching profession shortly after our interview. He was a brilliant first-year high school physics teacher. He was harassed mercilessly by students and teachers alike, and his pain was evident throughout his interview. He never admitted to anyone at school that he was gay, but he had a rainbow sticker on his car.

Peggy was thinking of leaving the teaching profession because she wanted to come out more publicly. Her partner was already out in her non-education-related workplace, and Peggy envied the effects of such freedom. She wondered aloud why there is such repression in the Florida school system.

Mary Lou has been a teacher at a specialized public school in northeast Florida for more than 2 decades. She and her partner of many years have children and grandchildren. She knows many teachers who are lesbian or gay, but says "no one talks about it." She herself has no desire to be open about her sexual orientation for fear of job loss.

Erik and his partner of 6 years are teachers in different northeast Florida districts. Erik's partner did not wish to be interviewed. Erik described himself and his partner as "extremely closeted." Although he expressed concern for lesbian and gay adolescents, he said he and his partner think that in northeast Florida "it's just too risky" to do anything. They certainly do not see themselves as needing to be role models. Erik said they are good teachers and enjoy their jobs, and wish to remain employed.

While all of the other participants invited me into their homes for their interviews, Rita asked to meet me in my home instead of her own. She is single and has two teenage children. Although she said her children know she's a lesbian, she did not want them to overhear our conversation. Rita is teaching in the school in which she grew up. She was in a school in another northeast Florida district but was indirectly and weakly accused of having an affair with a female student. The accusations were never substantiated, and, unlike Elisa's case, were never made public. She left that district and returned to her home district where she says she is much happier. She also said that although she is extremely closeted, she is fearful that such accusations could re-emerge, simply because of her sexual identity.

THEIR LIVES AND THEIR EXPERIENCES

Awareness of a Homosexual Orientation

Signorile (1995, ix) described being out of the closet as not having to worry any longer about one's sexual orientation being discovered. He stated that living in secret, living in the closet, prohibits people from living "a full, rewarding life and forces them to live in fear and shame."

None of the participants in this study considered themselves to be out of the closet other than with selected friends and family members, and all worried about the fear of discovery and subsequent job loss.

Participants were asked when they were first aware of their sexual orientation. Fourteen said they were aware of a sense of difference by the time they were in high school. Two of the 14 said they were at least partly open about their sexual orientation while they were teenagers. One woman described her high school years as being difficult because of her sexual orientation:

I knew by the time I was in high school. I feel like I had a lot of pain around my sexual orientation. I just kept trying with men. It just never worked. It was a very difficult time. Adolescence was not fun.

One of the male participants agreed:

I do not look back on it with fond memories. I don't cherish the time when I was young at all. I'm glad it's over. I feel so pained for my students because I know they have to go through the same thing.

Two teachers came out after having been in the northeast Florida school system for several years. Both had fallen in love with colleagues in their school settings.

Summary. The participants who were aware of their sexual orientation since adolescence reported being somewhat if not entirely closeted during that developmental period. For some, the years of being secretive about their sexual orientation spanned four or more decades. The length of awareness did not affect the participants' level of concern regarding others in their schools who might learn of their sexual orientation. All experienced and verbalized fear of discovery. That theme permeated every topic area in every interview. Further, none of the participants felt that this theme was unusual for educators in northeast Florida. These data assisted in establishing the framework for what became the filter of fear through which these participants view their students, colleagues, supervisors, and community.

Why Become a Teacher

Kissen (1996a) noted that lesbian and gay people, like most of their heterosexual colleagues, become teachers because of a desire to help young people. The dominance of this construct in the data justified the central placement of the "filter of fear" within the model. Through her studies, Kissen learned that most lesbian and gay teachers care deeply about children, have a love for ideas, and enjoy sharing those ideas with others. Like their heterosexual counterparts, lesbians and gay men become teachers for reasons that have nothing to do with their sexual orientation. Because of the pressures of homophobia that gay and lesbian teachers ultimately encounter, being a teacher becomes problematic for many of them.

Most of the participants in this study said they became teachers because they wanted to help young people learn and grow. An awareness of their homosexual orientation did not prevent them from becoming teachers. Their responses echoed Kissen's (1996a) findings:

I wanted to help other people. I wanted to make a difference in the lives of young people. I went into teaching with the idea that I could help people, without thinking much about my sexual orientation. I have something to give. I have a teaching philosophy and a love of teaching that really allows kids to learn. It is a good profession because it allows you the ability to serve, to give.

None of the participants expressed an awareness of potential difficulty as they were making the decision to become teachers. The common theme was a lack of information or understanding of what being lesbian or gay meant in the educational work setting: "I really didn't think about it. I didn't think it would be a problem. Knowing what I know now, I wouldn't recommend any lesbian or gay person go into teaching."

Summary. Most of the teachers in this study were aware of their homosexual orientation prior to becoming teachers. Their reasons for becoming teachers were similar to those of their heterosexual counterparts. These teachers were cognizant that they had compartmentalized their vocation and their sexual orientation completely and with great stress; they kept their work lives and their personal lives separate and disconnected—a task their heterosexual colleagues generally do not have to undertake.

The data regarding compartmentalization, separateness, and disconnection appear in the model as the foundation for experiences of these gay and lesbian teachers. The field of isolation of the teachers underscores the separateness from their colleagues and community that the participants described.

The Lesbian and Gay Community

Most of the participants in this study described the lesbian and gay community in northeast Florida as closeted, splintered, and unsupportive. Ironically, the northeast Florida area, especially Jacksonville, has a large, visible, organized lesbian and gay community, with institutions spanning many years. They include the Lesbian and Gay Community Association of Jacksonville (LGCAJ), Parents and Friends of Lesbians and Gays (PFLAG), the Metropolitan Community Church, the Jacksonville Area Sexual Minority Youth Network (JASMYN), the large Jacksonville Lesbian and Gay Chorus, the Pride Committee, and even Bo's Coral Reef—the oldest lesbian and gay night club in continuous existence in the state of Florida. With these organizations and others, most of the educators in this study felt estranged from the lesbian and gay community.

We don't know who we are or how many of us there are. We don't help each other at all. I'm not saying who's to blame. There's no blame at all. I am very closeted and not wanting anyone to find out. I was scared to death. We're so much shrouded in fear as a people. I had learned fear from people, learned that you don't say anything and you don't ask about it. We shut each other out. The lesbian and gay community here is very closeted.

For gay and lesbian teachers, this may be true. A Gay Lesbian Straight Educators Network (GLSEN) chapter was founded in northeast Florida in the fall of 1997 by a high school teacher who encountered problems with a school board member because the teacher was gay. He and his partner left northeast Florida to teach in Atlanta. A member of the GLSEN chapter who is at the University of North Florida offered this account:

Yes, there's a GLSEN chapter but no public school teachers attend meetings Teachers aren't any more open now than before. I know the problem of harassment of students is prevalent. I don't talk to public school teachers about their sexuality. It's very difficult to do that here. It's really not an issue because everyone is quite in the closet. I think if there is a future for GLSEN in northeast Florida, it will be with straight and gay-friendly folks who want to help their students. It is just too anathema for teachers to come out and deal with homophobia in their schools. (Personal email communication, January 1999).

The teachers in this study said they feel isolated, alone, and unaware of a large cohesive community of lesbian and gay people, even though several participants spoke of attending events within the gay and lesbian community. The people who make up the large lesbian and gay community are generally perceived by the participants in this study to be disconnected from one another and distrustful of each other, lacking in support or camaraderie.

The review of the literature did not yield research that examined how lesbian and gay teachers interact with the lesbian and gay community at large. There may be viable institutions in place for social relationships among lesbian and gay people in northeast Florida; however, the participants verbalized ideas that appear to conflict with the public appearance of the greater lesbian and gay community from whom they feel estranged. The model that represents the data collected in this study highlights participants' feelings of isolation from the lesbian and gay community.

Although both Harbeck (1992a) and Kissen (1996a) found that most gay and lesbian teachers in their studies were happy to locate and connect with other gay educators in their schools, the participants in this study did not feel the same way. They were not actively seeking out other lesbian and gay educators. In fact, they seemed to be extremely isolated from other lesbian and gay teachers, as depicted in the arrangements of components in the model.

Participants, however, did discuss how they found other gay teachers with whom to be friends or with whom to develop a support network in limited numbers. All described situations in which there is no system of support in place for them; further, none described an environment where they felt safe enough to initiate such a system.

We don't talk to each other. We don't support each other. I'm aware of at least 10 other teachers that are gay or lesbian in my school. But we don't sit around together, we don't discuss it at all. There really is no support. There are many of us, but we don't talk to each other very much. It would be great if just for one day all teachers, administrators, support personnel, and staff would come out. That would do a lot. There are a huge number of lesbians and gay men here. The American Federation of Teachers has a gay teachers' caucus, but we can't get it here. You can't even start one here because you'd have to officially come out. See, if I were to stand up and say I want to start this, I might as well say goodbye to my teaching career. I don't think it's safe enough to be in a support group here yet.

This teacher described the separation and isolation gay and lesbian educators experience from one another; although there are many gay and lesbian teachers, she saw no system of support available to them locally. The model represents this separation from gay and lesbian colleagues in the field of isolation.

One participant, a previous recipient of a Teacher of the Year award, added another dimension to the dynamics of these relationships. She expressed a reluctance to interact with other gay teachers. This educator spoke of a personal lack of respect for lesbian and gay teachers:

There are lots of gay teachers, but I'm torn between identifying with them because I don't respect them as much professionally. I know that there are some other teachers in my school who are gay, and the kids talk about them. Or the kids will come right out and tell you, "Well, he's queer" or "she's a lesbian." I don't know whether they don't have as much control in their classroom or as much respect from the kids because they're gay, or what. I'm not sure what the correlation is between knowing somebody's gay and gaining one's respect. I don't know if my students would respect me less if they knew that I were gay.

This award recipient said many gay and lesbian teachers throughout northeast Florida and the state have received the Teacher of the Year Award over the years. "They are just the best teachers you could possibly find. All of their energies go into their students." Curiously, although there was an acknowledgment that gay and lesbian teachers are "the best you could possibly find," this participant felt little respect for these teachers.

This participant demonstrated two conflicting but concurrently held viewpoints regarding lesbian and gay teachers as a group. First, the participant declared a lack of respect for them; then she said, "They are the best teachers" one could find. This type of conflictual thinking—evidencing a lack of respect yet acknowledging ability—is observed in both the gay and non-gay community. Such depersonalization of lesbian and gay people may arise from internalized homophobia. Finnegan and McNally (1987, 39) described this phenomenon:

Having to contend with the ever-present pressures of external homophobia on a day-to-day basis is, at best, demanding and disheartening. Dealing with internalized homophobia is more difficult and painful. As they grow up, most lesbians and gay men are taught the homophobic values of the culture. Gradually, they internalize these values—learn them, accept them as truth, and incorporate them into their belief system. After the lesbians and gay men realize they are homosexual, they apply these values to themselves because they are members of the stigmatized group. Many gays report growing up feeling uneasy about themselves, not sure what was "wrong," but sure "something" was indeed "wrong." As they began to sense or discovered how they were different, many were horrified to learn they belonged to a group reviled by this culture. The feelings generated by internalized homophobia are extremely painful. They are the feelings of a self divided. Many gay people feel the very center of their being is tainted and unacceptable. That which defines who they are becomes the enemy. Now they are beset by two hostile forces—from without and within.

This separation of self is seen repeatedly among the participants in this study.

Summary. All the participants expressed a belief that there is a large number of lesbian and gay teachers and administrators in northeast Florida. They believe there are neither methods of organization and support, nor a communication system for an informal network among them. All cited concern for personal safety, fear of discovery, and fear of job loss as the reasons for not actively developing a support network themselves. Their silence among one another implies a rule that prohibits discussing sexual orientation issues with or offering even casual support for one another. The model depicts this as an area in which participants do not feel safe enough to share information with their colleagues about their private lives, keeping the sense of isolation intact.

Methods of Communication among Lesbian and Gay Teachers

Stories about people who were harassed, humiliated, threatened, or fired from their teaching jobs solely because they were gay are somehow heard by every gay and lesbian teacher (Kissen, 1996a). Specific data from recent surveys reveal that 92% of gay and lesbian people have experienced verbal harassment and 24% have experienced physical abuse because of their sexual orientation (Herek, 1989).

The lesbian and gay educators of northeast Florida are familiar with such stories and statistics. Participants explained how gay and lesbian educators share information, even with their acknowledged lack of communication and support. Observation and third-person hearsay are the primary routes for transmitting information, as opposed to actual first-person experiences.

I was worried that people at my school would find out about me, because my principal would just have a cow. There's an openly gay man there now, and the principal doesn't like him. I heard he's leaving. The principal is not a good person to have as an enemy. He can make your life a living hell. I just couldn't stand the pressure he would put on me, like he did on that man.

The interpretive model represents this perception within the concentric circle. Here are found the people who participants believe have power over them because of their homosexual orientation. This report is an example of a teacher perceiving the principal though the filter of fear of job loss. Such fear creates a powerful need for teachers to maintain their isolation from others in the school setting.

Pivotal events remain fresh in the minds and in the stories passed on from teacher to teacher, even though the events may have occurred in the distant past. An example shared by more than one participant was a police raid on the City Bath Club in Jacksonville more than 20 years ago. According to these storytellers, the Jacksonville newspaper published the names of the people arrested at the club. One participant commented, "There were pretty prominent people's names on the list. People who were teachers lost their jobs."

Other teachers reported that they obtain their information from what they intuitively sense in addition to what they observe about their schools, their communities, and their counties. Some of the participants in this study recalled having had that intuition when they were students. One teacher described how this process develops:

I knew when I was in high school that I had lesbian teachers, and I knew that there was fear. I knew that I couldn't say anything to them. There is such a division. There are a lot of teachers who feel so strongly against lesbian and gay teachers that you don't talk about it. I've seen too many Ander Crenshaw (Republican politician from Jacksonville known to be anti-gay) bumper stickers at my school. I know to keep my mouth shut and my eyes and ears open.

Summary. The model depicts this intuitive process only indirectly. Participants do not feel safe enough to share information with their colleagues about their private lives, so they keep the sense of isolation intact, as shown in the arrangement of components on the field of isolation.

The participants in this study described communication processes among lesbian and gay teachers which are very similar to the methods by which events are communicated in every community: Observation, personal experience, and both written and oral history shape what community members know about their environment. Gay individuals more typically learn about their environment from people who heard about events but not directly involved. It would appear that information carrying strong affect is transmitted by accounts of either real or imagined events, with intuition guiding the process of any behavior change. Throughout many of the accounts is a verbalization demonstrating the incorporation of a very strong message that public schools in northeast Florida are not safe for either gay and lesbian teachers or students.

The Lives of Gay and Lesbian Teachers

Lesbian and gay teachers who are closeted at work are less satisfied with their interpersonal interactions and experience stress around sexual orientation issues (Juul & Repa, 1993). Kissen (1996a, 38) talked about the paradox of oppression:

Creating safer schools for gay teachers and students means building alliances with educators from other targeted [minority] groups. Yet therein lies the unique paradox of gay oppression. Reaching out to a straight ally means becoming visible as a lesbian or gay teacher. And while lesbian and gay educators know that hiding is what keeps homophobia in place, for most of them it is still a way of life.

Participants discussed their own reluctance to reach out to anyone in the public school system in northeast Florida and acknowledged that by their silence they, too, are responsible for maintaining a homophobic environment.

When asked directly what it is like to be a gay or lesbian teacher in northeast Florida, their responses were very similar. One teacher offered a response that mirrored that of nearly every other participant:

Oppressive. It's oppressive. It's not open, it's not free. There's nothing liberating about it. Being a teacher in this county is tough to begin with. Being a lesbian just adds to the worries. It just makes you always watch your step because you know that if something happens, and someone has the ability to dig up your life, they're going to use it against you like it was some sort of a crime, which in the state of Florida, it still is.

One teacher said she felt "absolutely no degree of comfort" about being a lesbian and a teacher in northeast Florida:

I'm pretty much scared all the time. It's a major stress that takes away from the love and skill of teaching. I hate this. It's very tough.

One participant lost his partner of more than 20 years when the partner was murdered in a gay-bashing incident. The participant described his experience and the cloak of silence around his loss.

When my partner was killed, that was a very difficult year—the circumstances under which he died and the pressure I was under, and the fact that my partner was gone. He had been missing for two days. They found his body on a Monday, and I didn't go back to school until the following Monday. I didn't dare share the information with anyone at school. They didn't know I was gay or know anything about the life we had together. Luckily, I had a family doctor who was able to get me out of school for a week. But it's like I had to walk into work as though nothing had happened. I had to grieve and hide at the same time. I didn't know what to do. It was extremely difficult. You just go through it, pretending as if nothing is wrong. My life-mate died and I had to pretend he never existed. That was several years ago. They still don't know at school.

Summary. The participants in this study reported a lack of the ordinary social support systems available to others in the workplace. Without such support, they expressed a confusion about how to behave and in whom to confide when a crisis occurred. Fear, stress, and isolation appeared to be constant and daily aspects of functioning for these educators. For the individuals in this study, being a lesbian or gay teacher in northeast Florida is frightening, oppressive, lonely, and very difficult. The model depicts the loneliness though the emotional separation of participants from the others with whom they must daily interact and from whom they might, under other circumstances, enjoy support.

Interactions with Colleagues and Supervisors

The literature reveals more information regarding lesbian and gay teachers' interactions with students than with colleagues or supervisors. Most of the participants in this study described discomfort with colleagues and distrust of their principals and administrators. One teacher expressed the discomfort that would accompany any query about sexual orientation:

I don't know what I would do if my principal asked me if I was a lesbian. I'd have to say no. I know from my own experience that people will immediately hate me. Nobody in my school knows about me. It's just not safe. There are a lot of teachers who feel so strongly against lesbian and gay teachers that you don't talk about it. I've seen too many bumper stickers for Christian Coalition candidates at my school. I just don't discuss things with other teachers or administrators.

When participants discussed support systems for gay or lesbian teachers within the public school system, they noted no significant contributions from colleagues or supervisors. As one teacher commented:

I don't know of any examples of support I can give to you. I can't imagine there being any genuine support, not from the administration of my school or from the school board.

In addition to feeling a lack of support, lesbian and gay teachers in this study reported feeling fearful of administrators. This concern appeared in several excerpts above in which teachers described how principals might react if their sexual orientation became known. Several of the teachers even suggested that until the laws in Florida change to prevent job termination because of one's homosexual orientation, positive interaction with colleagues and supervisors would be impossible.

These teachers expressed a distrust of colleagues that they thought prevented the formation of work-related friendships. A self-imposed alienation from colleagues and supervisors appeared to exist among nearly all of the participants and appears as part of the second concentric circle in the model. One participant acknowledged the safety of the closet: "Being a gay teacher who is closeted affords some people the silence they need. It's a good place to hide. But sometimes you just get tired of hiding."

Summary. None of the participants clearly described what kind of administrative support for lesbian and gay people would be desirable. They articulated an overall problem with discrimination, but did not know what to do to obtain support in order to cope or to make change. Full participation with colleagues, both in the work environment and socially, was reported to be "hopeless." None of these teachers was able to verbalize a process for change beyond wishing that change would occur.

Parents of Students

Kissen (1996b, 223) stated that lesbian and gay teachers have become the primary political targets of the radical right. She noted that it has been easy for some groups to manipulate parents' legitimate concerns for their children's safety. Such concern "plays into the public debate over sex education, a debate that in turn touches on Americans' deepest anxieties and depressions." Kissen (1996a, 76) also noted that educators thought pressure to have teachers fired would more likely come from the communities in which they worked than from colleagues or administrators. Parents were perceived to be the ones who most often apply such pressure. Indeed, "the influence of parental opinion is so strong in most communities that even teachers with supportive administrators wonder how long the support would last in the face of community pressure." The participants' concerns in this study reflected Kissen's findings. One teacher hypothesized:

Parents would probably get upset if they knew I was a lesbian. I think that would be the main reason the principal would get upset. If a parent raised a stink, they would have to do something, fire me, reprimand me or start a procedure, depending on what the parent would want. It just depends on what the parent would want. Parents have all the power. Parents in my school are just so consumed with anti-gay sentiment. If they thought their son or daughter was being taught by a homosexual, they'd go to the school board and raise such holy hell.

Summary. None of the teachers in this study perceived the parents of their students to be allies. They explained that they believe parents have the influence to transfer or fire them. For public school teachers, interpersonal meetings with parents are typical in classroom situations, yet few participants spoke of such interactions with parents. One inference from this view of parents is that these teachers avoid one-to-one meetings with their students' parents. One teacher said such meetings occurred only when the child was a disciplinary problem, and added that parents of such children were usually "as bad as their kid." All of the teachers in this study articulated a belief that parents of students have control over their careers; with this assertion, they placed parents in the same circle on the model as students, colleagues, and supervisors. That is, the teachers perceived all of these groups as having power over them. Such perception established firmly their filters of fear.

Relationships with Students

The review of related literature revealed little that discusses the relationship of lesbian and gay teachers to the general student population in their schools. Although all of the participants in this study became teachers because of their desire to work with young people, all described strained relationships and self-imposed distance from their students. Several spoke of attitudes and actions they personally experienced or observed among students in their schools.

I find where it gets sticky for me is when they ask about your personal life, if I'm married, things like that. It would bother me a lot if the kids know about me. They're the ones who can be mean, nasty, and do the damage.

The perception of students having power over teachers may be a trigger for activation of the fear filter in the model that then affects teachers' behaviors and attitudes. It is through this filter, or screen, that interactions with students take place.

Several participants who teach in the lower grades shared their feelings about being physical with their students, especially since many of the younger students need and give hugs. One teacher expressed her anxiety in reference to hugging her young students, but felt that the hug was more important than her fear:

These kids need hugs and I give them when they need them. The kid always initiates it, though. I don't initiate it at all. If a kid's going to hug me, I'm not going to turn my back on them at all. Sometimes I worry about that, but I really don't feel like I have a choice. I am careful about it and it makes me nervous to give hugs. It does.

However, others were more cautious.

There are so many rules and regulations shoved down our throats that I'm afraid to deal with these kids, to touch them the way I'd like to, the way they need, but I'm too afraid. We are told very emphatically, you will not ever touch a student, even if a student might need this [touches my lower arm in a gentle fashion] to ask if you're okay today.

These teachers lamented their inability to interact with students as heterosexual teachers do. Once again, the filter of fear is evident because they worry that their actions of caring might be misinterpreted and their positions jeopardized.

Teachers interact with students in a variety of settings, during both class sessions and extracurricular activities. The fear of misinterpretation arises in all situations. A teacher used to have parties for members of school clubs in her home, an activity typical of heterosexual colleagues. She said she would never do it again: "I would never dream of having a club party in my home now. I wouldn't do that. I did it when I was a younger teacher, but I wouldn't do it now. It's much too risky." Other teachers also felt that parties and after-school group activities with students were potentially troublesome, and they rarely participated.

Summary. The lesbian and gay teachers in this study expressed deep anxiety about answering questions students normally ask all teachers about their private lives. They projected an exaggerated fear of accusations of child molestation; therefore, each devised creative mechanisms to prevent that possibility, while sacrificing the opportunity for closeness with their students. The filter of fear in the model stands between these teachers and their students. These participants went to the extreme to ensure career safety at the cost of human warmth and an expression of caring towards students that are traditionally associated with teachers.

Relationships with Gay and Lesbian Students

Gay and lesbian adolescents are a population at an elevated risk for intra- and interpersonal problems when compared to non-gay adolescents (Walling, 1996, 11).

With little recognition, few resources, and minimal support, they are an at-risk population too often ignored by administrators, teachers, and counselors who are unaware, uninformed, or uncomfortable with same-sex closeness. The price of our ignorance can be fatal.

A Federal Task Force Report on Youth Suicide (Gibson, 1989) documented that adolescents struggling with sexual orientation issues committed more than a third of all teen suicides. Young people dealing with their sexual orientation need role models and stories about people who struggled with similar issues and survived. Their lesbian and gay teachers could be such role models, but fear of exposure keeps teachers silent. It is unknown whether some of these teen suicides could have been prevented if they had had teachers who were open about their sexual orientation and comfortable in being available to talk with students in need.

The participants talked about experiences with their own gay and lesbian students.

They look at you and they know they're not supposed to say anything. These kids are beat up. It's just so unfair. By the time they get to the age where they can accomplish something, they feel so bad about themselves it takes the rest of their lives to deal with it.

Such observations reflect an understanding of the primary developmental task for lesbian and gay adolescents. The adolescent must achieve an "adjustment to a socially stigmatized role in isolation without adequate, honest information about themselves or others who are like them during a time of tremendous physical, social, emotional, and intellectual change" (Harbeck, 1992a, 13).

Uribe and Harbeck (1992, 11) admonished that "cultural taboos, fear of controversy, and a deeply rooted, pervasive homophobia have kept the educational system in the United States blindfolded and mute on the subject of homosexuality." They warned that lesbian and gay young people face a high risk of rejection, abuse, drug use, homelessness, prostitution, and suicide because all educators, homosexual and heterosexual alike, "breached their ethical and professional obligations by being uninformed and unresponsive" to the needs of lesbian and gay adolescents.

They also noted that support systems created to serve all other populations of young people are not available in appropriate forms to serve the
needs of lesbian and gay adolescents. The same reasons that prevent
these students from being served, prevent lesbian and gay educators from
serving.

Gay and lesbian educators believe that a strict separation between their personal
and professional lives is required and that to be publicly "out" at school would
cost them their jobs. Thus, they describe themselves as constantly vigilant about
protecting their secret identities, and the energy required to maintain this false
public facade takes a tremendous psychological toll. This fear affects relationships with colleagues, students, and parents, creating a sense of isolation for the
educator. Finally, these teachers experience frustration about changing the public's negative image of lesbian and gay people to match their own sense of
themselves as worthy people and good teachers. (Griffin, 1992a, 168)

These lesbian and gay educators described how they interacted with
lesbian and gay students within such a complex situation. Participants
spoke of their great reluctance to have more than a typical classroom relationship with their presumed gay-identified students. They lamented
their perceived inability to be role models and allies not only for all students, but also especially for gay and lesbian students. These educators
described a desire to help students, but expressed the overriding fear of
job loss. One teacher's reflection portrays the dilemma:

Basically, kids can pass. That's what I had to do. I'm dying to help a kid. I want
to come out. Am I afraid of losing my job? Yes. Is it worth it? No. The shame of
it is that we allow it to happen. I really want to get to a place to be able to do
something for these kids, because I went through hell getting where I am, you
know, and I hate to think that every generation has to go through the same thing.
These kids are experiencing the same thing I did when I was young. They already know that you're not supposed to let anybody know. They already know
the rules.

Some of these educators described what goes through their minds
when they view their classrooms and sense that lesbian and gay students
are looking to them for guidance. One teacher "quietly hoped" that she is
a good role model as a lesbian, but, because she is not out about her sexual orientation, she is unable to accomplish that goal. This account provides yet another example where a lesbian or gay individual verbalized
an observed need, but thought he or she was unable to implement the
action required to correct that need. Another teacher noted:

I would love to help them, but I can't. They have nowhere to go. These kids are going through the same thing I went through at their age and it's hell to watch. I want to tell them to hang in there, to survive. But I can't.

Lesbian and gay youth who need role models in the schools of northeast Florida will find no one. One teacher explained the decisions of such teachers by describing the context in which they teach and the rules of the local school boards and the community:

Four words are verboten in northeast Florida: *homosexuality, masturbation, abortion* and *AIDS*. You say those words and you're out of a job. These are words, and if you talk about them in any context other than the Bible, your job is on the line. No wonder these kids are at risk.

The rules that forbid the use of the four identified words appear to be local and common to the five northeast Florida school districts, although actual documentation of this prohibition was not forthcoming during the research for this work. Although some specific sexual behaviors are considered to be profane according to Florida law (Florida Statutes, 1995h), no statute appears to forbid the use of the words *AIDS, abortion*, or *homosexuality* in the public schools. The word *masturbation* is, however, considered to be profane (Florida Statute, 1995h). The other words—*AIDS, abortion, homosexuality*—are likely used, or had their use discontinued, in a variety of contexts based on the curriculum choice of local school districts throughout Florida. The participants in this study verbalized belief that the school districts in northeast Florida are more restrictive than the districts in western or southern Florida.

The review of the literature did not reveal a description of forbidden terms by the local school boards of northeast Florida, although such documentation may exist. It was extremely difficult to obtain information directly from these school districts. For example, none of the school district offices in northeast Florida responded to repeated requests by telephone, mail, and personal visits for a copy of the brochure entitled the *Code of Ethics and the Principles of Professional Conduct of the Education Profession in Florida* (Florida Statutes, 1995a, b). It was through the World Wide Web sites of WJXT Channel 4 in Jacksonville and the Florida Supreme Court in Tallahassee that documentation was finally obtained, and a lesbian administrators who knew I was searching for it finally located one and sent it to me.

Within this type of setting, the lesbian and gay teachers in this study reported that they understood the experiences of their lesbian and gay students, and verbalized that their own uncomfortable history was being repeated. When participants considered how they might be helpful to lesbian and gay adolescents, the subject of role models arose once again. In one teacher's view,

> We could be role models if it were safe. These kids have no other outlet. They don't know who else is gay. That's what's so painful, I mean, so painful to not be able to come out at school knowing that kids are suffering and I could prevent that suffering. Gay and lesbian young people do need role models. They do need heroes. They do need to see that despite the fact that they're confused and we are very discriminated against, you can still achieve greatness in this world, be somebody, make a difference, not in just one person's life, but maybe in hundreds of thousands of peoples' lives. But it's still not a good thing to be gay or lesbian here.

Summary. The participants stated a desire to acknowledge lesbian and gay students and to assist them, but they expressed an unwillingness to be available for fear of discovery and ultimate job loss. They commented that they still feel the pain and fear that they had experienced as gay teenagers themselves 10, 20, 30, and more years ago. All the teachers in this study stated that they believe gay and lesbian adolescents in northeast Florida are an at-risk population who need to be acknowledged and assisted, but that they were unable to identify who would be the role models and advocates for these children. They are unable to pass through their filter of fear in the model to interact with lesbian and gay youth, a subset of the gay and lesbian community from which they remain isolated. The situations described in this section also act as vehicles for encouraging gay and lesbian youth to develop their own filters of fear, thereby passing the filter to another generation.

Advocacy for Gay and Lesbian Youth

Lesbian and gay adolescents are children who, like all other children, have a right to be safe in their schools. Harbeck (1995, 133) underscored the importance of having advocates for gay and lesbian youth. Advocates would support students in attaining both their rights and opportunities to grow and develop.

Lesbian, gay, and bisexual concerns are a civil rights issue, a humanitarian concern, a question of fairness, equity, equal protection, and of valuing diversity and individual differences. They are a question of developing human potential and creativity, of making unique contributions, and of broadening our traditionally held views on gender roles, love, commitment, the family, and sexuality. Teachers struggle every day to teach students calculus, or English literature, or American history. What, however, is the value of these subjects if your students are wounded by prejudice, suffer from low self-esteem and feelings of isolation, and are limited in their life opportunities by ignorance and discrimination?

One source for these advocates of gay and lesbian youth is the teaching staff in the schools.

Unfortunately, Kissen (1996a, 58) found that gay and lesbian teachers sometimes "acquiesce in the unjust treatment of gay students because of their own fears of being exposed." Although all the participants in this study expressed a desire to be advocates, they all said they were morbidly afraid of losing their jobs and unable to speak out. One teacher explained:

I'm too afraid. They'll fire me. I couldn't be an advocate. Not here. Not at this point. I don't think anyone could be an advocate unless they had a lot of support from the principal and administration. I don't see that working here. [But] I think we as lesbian and gay teachers would be great advocates for them if our jobs weren't on the line.

Even though these participants did not see themselves as advocates, they did note that they could assist these students in subtle ways.

You can be nice to them. You can say nice things to give a kid support. Or you might walk up to a kid and say, "It's going to be okay." In a subtle way, you have to let them know that they're going to make it.

One teacher offered a suggestion but decided it was merely a fantasy. "A support group at school might help. Maybe the counselors could initiate it. Oh, I guess that's just a dream in this county." None of the participants was willing to be a faculty advisor for a student support group without guarantees that their jobs would not be in jeopardy.

Summary. The educators in this study did not implement their desire to be advocates for lesbian and gay students for fear of the discovery of their own sexual orientation and resulting job loss. Furthermore, the examples of possible advocacy that they offered seemed to be wishes upon which they would not act. The model shows the isolation these teachers experience because they are unable to reach out as advocates to their gay and lesbian students. Their inaction portrays how solid the filter of fear can become. Teachers who identify with the plight of these lesbian and gay students refrain from interaction with them that would both instruct and support; in a sense, the teachers model fear for their students.

Teaching Lesbian and Gay History

Teaching history is one of the methods by which young members of society learn the common culture. If such teaching is to be complete, it is necessary to include lesbian and gay individuals and events in secondary schools (Lipkin, 1995, 40).

If our mission in schools is to cultivate our students' interest in truth and to give them the skills to begin to search for it, this kind of intentional ignorance [omitting lesbian and gay history from the curriculum] through censorship runs counter to our goal. It may be that, some years ago, we could honestly say that scholarship was spotty on the subject of homosexuality, and good sources of material were not available. Today the thriving pursuit of gay studies on the university level provides volumes of respected research and exciting theory.

An opportunity for all students to learn and understand about diversity to its broadest extent is lost when lesbian and gay people and events are not included in the curriculum.

The participants in this study acknowledged that they were unable to be visible role models for lesbian and gay students. They also reported being uncomfortable teaching about lesbian and gay heroes as a means of providing indirect role models. Strikingly, in addition to being fearful, most of these teachers were unable to teach gay and lesbian history primarily because they reported being unfamiliar with many significant events and people. For example, they reported that they did not know about the impact of the Harlem Renaissance, the Nazis' devastation of gay and lesbian people, and the recent decision overturning Colorado's Amendment Two by the United States Supreme Court. They also reported being unaware of the well-documented homosexuality of people throughout history, such as Plato, King James, Leonardo da Vinci, Cole Porter, Peter Tschaikovsky, computer inventor Alan Turing, Margaret Mead, Walt Whitman, Bill Tilden, Gertrude Stein, James Baldwin, and many others.

Mentioning the homosexual orientation of famous people during the course of class discussion is the most common method of including lesbian and gay people and issues in the curriculum (Walling, 1996). One participant did teach about lesbian and gay individuals by incorporating the information into his regular lessons. He explained:

I want them to know. I don't know how many other people tell them these stories. I know, so subjects like James [the] First being gay or Mary Stewart's husband being gay would probably not enter into their teaching. I mention it, but I do it in such a way to get the information across without being revelatory about myself.

Another teacher wished she could do the same.

I could provide role models for students. I could say to the lesbian or gay kid in my classroom who's thinking he or she is the only one, suddenly there are role models, somebody who's kind of famous. The kids might then think they're not as awful as they're feeling, and not as alone. Maybe they'll survive. Maybe I'll do it someday.

None of the other participants in this study reported being as bold or as informed. One teacher was asked if he talked about lesbian and gay issues in his classroom. He remarked: "In class? Oh, heck, no. No, I would never do that. I would never do that, basically because I don't want to rock the boat."

Several participants spoke of the tactics they use to maneuver around the implied restrictions that forbid teachers to share information with students about AIDS, abortion, or sexual orientation. One teacher described her approach:

I always carry AIDS information with me. For example, I always carry the little cards [from the Public Health Department] with the AIDS numbers so if kids have questions about AIDS, I leave the card sitting on the side of the desk. I take the kid aside and say, "I can't give you these numbers. I want you to copy them down. If someone finds them, you didn't get them from me." I kind of go the extra mile when I'm not supposed to, but I risk my job every time.

Florida law (Florida Statutes, 1995j, section s) describes in specific language the various types of courses in which AIDS education should be taught. Schools will "teach abstinence from sexual activity outside of marriage as the expected standard for all school-age children while teaching the benefits of monogamous heterosexual marriage." The tone of this language nullifies the value of sexually active unmarried heterosexual and homosexual people; the consequences of such omissions can be far-reaching and have a long-term negative impact upon society.

Summary. Some teachers in this study described violating local school board policy occasionally to talk with any of their students, gay or straight, who need information about sexual orientation and other sensitive issues. They said they were aware of the risks, but were willing to take them in limited amounts in order to provide information to their students. However, most participants in this study did not report taking such risks, once again citing fear of discovery and ultimate job loss. In this example, students, colleagues, parents of students, and the school board as shown in the model work in tandem to activate the filter of fear. Due to the apparent prohibitive nature of school board policies, local climate, and their own limited knowledge base, they reported that they do not provide valuable information to their students.

Culture of the Community

An important area for discussion in the interviews was the culture of the communities in which the participants live and work. When each described a political or religious climate rather than a culture, the participant was encouraged to elaborate. All agreed that the Northeast Florida area is highly conservative, politically dominated by the First Baptist Church and the Christian Coalition, and perceived to be generally unfriendly toward lesbian and gay people. One person shared:

We're living in a city that's very conservative. Northeast Florida is the Bible Belt's seat of intolerant ignorance. For a community that prides itself on Christian principles like tolerance, they are very unchristian. Northeast Florida is a terrible place to teach in. I'll tell that to anybody. It's a horrible place. This area is so behind.

Another teacher added a similar description:

My experience is that the attitude of this community toward lesbians and gay people ranges from mild disgust to hostility. This is the Bible Belt of the South here. They're pretty narrow-minded here.

Another participant also acknowledged the influence of the First Baptist Church and its accompanying Christian Coalition connection:

This is such a Bible Belt, Christian Coalition, hell, fire, and brimstone type of community, totally run by the Baptist Church. That's just the way it is here. You've got the First Baptist Church downtown that owns half the city. So we're living in the Dark Ages here. The really sad part is we have school board members who are deacons in the First Baptist Church, and all of the people who want promotions go to the First Baptist Church. I don't know where the superintendent goes to church, but I assume if it's not the Baptist Church downtown, it's a Baptist church somewhere. Or now it could even be the Episcopal Church with that bigoted new bishop.

Several participants shared that they feel unsafe and see safety as an issue for the lesbian and gay students in the schools in which they teach. Two who are partners were considering leaving the northeast Florida area. One commented:

I don't want to be constantly scared or afraid of discrimination or violence or something like that. I don't want people hating me for who I love. I want to be able to be proud of it, openly proud. To try to do it here would be looking for trouble, looking for someone to be violent against us, that sort of thing. I'm too concerned about our safety. It's not safe. It would be impossible for anyone to come out in my school. Students would be crazy to come out. They'd probably get killed by their peers.

Participants spoke of the terminology occasionally used by other teachers towards students in spite of the fact that the *Code of Ethics and the Principles of Professional Conduct of the Education Profession in Florida* (Florida Statutes, 1995a, b) prohibits such behavior.

Take the word *nigger*, for example. If you use the word *nigger*, you're in deep shit. I know teachers who've had their licenses suspended for three or four months and had to attend multicultural classes and all this other stuff. But nothing happens if teachers use the words *queer* or *faggot*.

Summary. All of the participants perceived northeast Florida to be an unsafe, intolerant, conservative area. A heterosexual school administrator, who identified as a member of the First Baptist Church, stated that the church is intolerant of gays and lesbians and teaches an extremely conservative perspective (personal communication, October 25, 1996). Nearly every participant expressed both anger and fear toward organized religion, especially the large First Baptist Church and its position regarding gays and lesbians. Indeed, the participants' attitudes toward and about the First Baptist Church as the embodiment of all fundamental religious organizations seem to influence strongly their concept of culture in the northeast Florida area. The model represents the participants' understanding of the local climate. The outer circle of the model depicts the perceived power of the fundamentalist religious organizations.

Community Socializing

Participants discussed how they socialize in the northeast Florida area. They described whether they attend functions in the lesbian and gay community, whether they go to events at their schools, or whether they attend parties given by colleagues or supervisors. There is little in the literature that describes these social experiences of lesbian and gay educators.

Nearly half of the teachers in this study said they do not socialize in the northeast Florida area at all. They prefer to go to cities such as Atlanta or Orlando for dining, dancing, and other social activities. The fear of meeting students or colleagues in public settings—such as movie theaters, concert halls, or gathering places such as the Jacksonville Landing or Metropolitan Park—in the company of one's partner or date, forced participants to socialize elsewhere or not at all. One teacher shared a circumstance that occurred on the day of our interview:

Today, my partner went to an event downtown. My school is near there and I'm sure probably most of my kids are there today. There's just no way I would go there. My partner went without me. It's too risky. It's not worth it to ruin my career.

One participant shared that she and her partner celebrated Gay Pride Day in Atlanta:

I was reading about the Gay Pride week festivities in Jacksonville. We should be going there, not Atlanta, but I'm afraid to take the chance. We should be supporting the cause in northeast Florida. But it's too scary. We're real careful. We go out of town a lot so we don't have to be paranoid when we're trying to have a nice time.

One teacher, who is single, spoke of not socializing at all: "Being a teacher and being gay has hampered my ability to have a social life. God, yes. I don't have one, a social life. That's got to be unhealthy." This young man held feelings similar to those of the other participants: He was uncomfortable with the possibility of running into students or colleagues in any social setting, and therefore chose not to socialize at all. He explained that he did not attend events at school because he was tired of both students and colleagues "harassing" him about not having a girlfriend.

Summary. The interpretive model represents this separation by locating the educational community to which teachers relate in a field of isolation. Few people in this study participate in social events at their schools or with colleagues. They either avoid these events, appear alone, or bring a "cover-up" date of the opposite sex. Such events often produce a great amount of stress for the participants, especially if they have partners. Participants offered some perspective on this behavior by noting that it is difficult to imagine a heterosexual teacher giving second thought as to whether or not she or he should bring her or his spouse or opposite-sex date to school-related events.

Lesbian and gay teachers in this study verbalized high levels of stress, isolation, and fear of discovery. They were not confident that their colleagues would support and protect them if they later became aware of the participants' sexual identities. These educators continued to express their overriding fear of the potential loss of employment if their homosexual orientations were discovered. Further, the interaction between fear and isolation is mutually reinforcing.

Climate in the Schools

Zuckerman and Simons (1994, 15) described the climate of a workplace as that which defines how employees and customers will be treated. They designed a scale to determine workplace climate as it relates to lesbian and gay people. One end of the scale marks a "Cold and Forbidding" climate, which includes harassment or physical injury toward an individual or group; the other end of the scale marks a "Warm and Receptive" environment which reflects the consideration of sexual orientation issues as a normal part of the workplace. All participants in this study described their schools in terms of what Zuckerman and Simons labeled "Cold and Forbidding." One teacher elaborated:

The climate of my school is ice cold, is not gay and lesbian friendly, to say the least. The climate in my school is very homophobic. Due to the oppression I feel, I do not socialize with my co-workers, and I eat my lunch in my room 95% of the time. The student body as well as their parents are decidedly intolerant. They have no room for difference in their lives. Just last week, a young man in my school was beaten up three times for being gay. Nobody stopped it.

Most participants provided similar descriptions of their schools. They all used the example of teachers not stopping the use of prejudicial language against gays and lesbians. They report that comments based on race were prohibited, but not prejudicial language based on sexual orientation.

A kid can call another kid a faggot or queer and nothing is said. But if they call them anything else, like a racial slur or anything like that, then they really deal with the problem. So the message is this: It seems to be quite alright for kids to use that kind of language, faggot, queer, dyke, that kind of thing.

Participants described a lack of sensitivity and knowledge of lesbian and gay issues and resources among most school counselors. Few participants said they would send a student to the school counselor if that student were dealing with sexual orientation issues. In fact, most participants commented that they believe there is no safe place or protective person in their schools for a lesbian or gay student.

The participants expressed how they personally experienced discomfort and threats in their work settings. Whereas few had experienced direct encounters, all feared that such encounters could occur. One individual described how the climate of an environment could lead to perceptions of a threat and how one might respond:

I've heard enough comments, not really about me but about lesbians and gays that tell me that I need to be quiet about it. That hurts me and it frightens me. I hear my colleagues saying negative things about gays or lesbians. We just learn to live with it. I heard a teacher not long ago, talk about so-and-so's son who's queerer than a three-dollar bill. I was right on the verge of saying something, but it wasn't worth the effort. It would have created more problems for me. I just can't speak out for these students or for myself. I'm beginning to wonder about feeling paranoid, but, when I have to go to school and have to walk around the 200 people who are doing daily Bible study around the flagpole to get to my classroom, the paranoia seems awfully real.

This account supports two areas of the interpretive model. Once again, teachers' fear of colleagues and their isolation from colleagues are stressed.

Participants explored the relationship between their awareness of potential threats and their ability to perform their duties as educators. One teacher implied a broad role for the teacher, a role beyond that of instructor in the classroom. However, acting on that role as a gay or lesbian educator risks too much:

I'm not allowed to express myself. I mean, it's really difficult. The other teachers are allowed to, can deal with the kids on a social level like outside of school and be very honest with them or deal with them after school, like a coach. I could never do that. I could never be, I just couldn't do it. I don't think anyone, student or teacher, could be out in the schools here unless they had a lot of support from the principal and administration. I don't see that happening. You want to reach out to these kids, but you don't for your own safety's sake.

This participant described a sense of separateness from her students and thereby placed the students in the circle that identifies those who have power over her life.

Summary. Overall, participants described their schools as being cold and unsafe for lesbian and gay teachers and students. They expressed anger directed at the climate that has created the fearful environment in which they work. They also expressed a sense of powerlessness and an inability to change the situation. The filter of fear, therefore, is partially based on anger and powerlessness.

Encounters with Discrimination at School

The state of Florida currently has no law that prohibits discrimination against lesbian and gay people; neither does it protect them in the areas of employment or housing. The southeastern Florida cities of Miami Beach and Key West and the counties of Broward and Palm Beach have local ordinances which offer limited protection in employment. The Florida Legislature recently added the term *sexual orientation* to the *Hate Crimes Reporting Act* (Florida Statutes, 1995i) and the Florida Criminal Code entitled *Evidencing Prejudice While Committing Offense* (Florida Statutes, 1995g). Protection from discrimination based on sexual orientation is not included in Florida's *Civil Rights Act* (Florida Statutes, 1995f) or in the *Florida Employment Policy* (Florida Statutes, 1995e).

The Florida Board of Education policy—The *Code of Ethics and the Principles of Professional Conduct of the Education Profession in Florida* (Florida Statutes, 1995a, b)—that is an available but rarely distributed brochure, prohibits sexual orientation discrimination and harassment by teachers against students. This nondiscrimination policy does not extend to employment in public education in Florida and offers no protection for teachers; however, it does offer limited protection for students provided it is enforced. Unfortunately, the educators who participated in this study reported that they are unfamiliar with this policy. The founder of the northeast Florida chapter of the Gay Lesbian Straight Educators Network (GLSEN) said that "teachers generally don't know about the policy until they violate it" (Ken Jackson, personal communication, January 18, 1999).

The newest teacher in the study said that a photocopy of the *Code of Ethics* section of the brochure was given to her when she began her studies as a new education major at the University of North Florida (UNF). However, the sexual orientation nondiscrimination policy is not contained in that section. It is in the *Principles of Professional Conduct of the Education Profession in Florida.* An advisor in the Office of Student Services at the University of North Florida's College of Education and Human Services in Jacksonville reported that UNF now distributes the actual brochure to new education majors, and students must sign a receipt indicating their intent to read it (Advisor, UNF College of Education and Health Services Office of Student Services, personal communication, October 25, 1996).

Participants recounted events that they saw as examples of discrimination in their schools. This included students discriminating against other students, students discriminating against teachers, teachers discriminating against students, and teachers discriminating against teachers. All said they had witnessed a variety of such discriminatory behaviors. Nearly all described examples of prejudicial language among all populations in their schools. Student-to-student slurs were most common, although nearly all participants said they occasionally hear students using such language towards teachers. Even though teachers in Florida's schools are prohibited from displaying discriminatory behavior or discriminatory language towards students (Florida Statutes, 1995b), participants reported frequently hearing other teachers refer to gay or lesbian students—or students perceived to be gay or lesbian—in a derogatory manner, often directly to the students themselves.

I've heard a couple of teachers in my school call some of the kids faggot or fairy. That is the most offensive thing to hear teachers calling students names. They do it all the time. *Faggot, sissy, dyke.* We're not there to call them names. They get enough of that at home. We have a lot of teachers at our school who think they are holier than thou.

Participants reported no observed consequences for such behavior by teachers, even though consequences are clearly defined in the *Code of Ethics and the Principles of Professional Conduct of the Education Profession in Florida* (Florida Statutes, 1995a, b).

One teacher described an incident in which drug program counselors were assigned to his school. Since he did "double duty" as a school counselor, the drug counselors spoke with him frequently. One of them told him that she is not allowed to talk with students about homosexuality, even if it directly relates to the drug problem and regardless of the severity of the drug problem.

Participants shared their own personal experiences with discriminatory language in their schools, either expressed by students or by colleagues or supervisors. One teacher recalled: "I invited my principal to come to the Walk for AIDS this year. She said, 'I'm not going on any queer walk.'"

Students also use discriminatory language, often more directly. One female teacher talked about an occasion when she had disciplined several students:

Yeah, I mean, they were calling me things like queer and lezzie because I was disciplining them. I can't go to my principal with that. Someone, they couldn't even spell it right, put on my door frame D-I-K-E. And a rock got thrown through my window, so I just covered the hole with a target.

Another teacher described the discriminatory behaviors of students. With tears in his eyes and his head lowered, one young teacher softly shared this story:

It would definitely create some problems if people knew I was gay. I'd be harassed and then I'd probably be fired. I guess I get harassed. I imagine you can consider it harassment. They call me queer. And I heard it. "He's a queer." My students called me a queer. They ask me all the time whether or not I have a girlfriend, and I'm like, no, I don't, and I don't want one. So they know, I think. They make comments all the time. I guess you would consider it harassment.

This teacher, who expressed a love for his students and an excitement about the difficult and technical subject he taught, left the teaching profession when the term ended and moved out of Florida.

Summary. The teachers in this study were in conflict between maintaining personal protection and "doing the right thing" by confronting discrimination. They stated they were unable to protect themselves or their students. The data collected in this study provided compelling evidence of discrimination, verbal harassment, and policy violation in some of the public schools in northeast Florida. The participants reported that such behavior toward lesbian and gay teachers and students makes the schools in northeast Florida unsuitable for teaching and learning. The participants' lack of familiarity with the only policy offering protection to lesbian and gay students in the public schools further exacerbates the situation. Its rules are neither acknowledged nor enforced, which underscores the lack of personal safety in these settings. This lack of safety and the evidence of discrimination and harassment act as triggers to accentuate the fear filter in the model.

When to Reveal One's Sexual Orientation

Teachers who must hide their sexual identity display three strategies for identity management (Woods & Harbeck, 1992). The strategies are (1) passing as heterosexual; (2) distancing oneself from colleagues, supervisors, and students; and (3) distancing oneself from issues of homosexuality. The participants in this study consistently described these strategies.

Participants described the extent to which they had revealed their sexual orientation in the context of the public school system. They also described with whom and under what conditions they have shared this information. None of the participants felt safe enough to share such information with individuals connected to the school environment. One teacher cited Florida's moral turpitude clause (Florida Statutes, 1995c) as a primary reason. She elaborated:

The Department of Education in the state of Florida has a moral turpitude clause. Now, they don't define moral turpitude. Moral turpitude loosely defined is that which is not of societal standard. This district will turn you in in a New York minute. My superintendent wasn't kidding when he recently said that his teachers won't go into bars. Because if you get drunk, whether you're driving or not, that's moral turpitude. God help you if you're sleeping with someone of the same sex.

Kissen (1996a, 44) described the process of the "Monday morning pronoun," which is similar to Woods and Harbeck's (1992) strategy of passing as heterosexual. Lesbian or gay teachers change the pronouns of the people with whom they spend time over the weekend, including their partners, in an attempt to appear heterosexual. Several of the participants in this study reported that they employ this technique to maintain their guise of heterosexuality and to avoid disclosure. One female teacher said this was her method of choice: "To prevent harassment, I refer to my partner as my husband. Nobody has any idea. Not a clue. There is no way to tell you how hard this is."

A second strategy involves distancing oneself from people (Woods & Harbeck, 1992). Several teachers described the tactics they employ to distance themselves from colleagues, supervisors, and students, especially when asked about personal information. One participant explained his elaborate distancing techniques:

I don't necessarily tell them I'm single. Sometimes I'll say I'm divorced, sometimes that I'm married and have three kids, two at a private school and one in college. I keep them guessing. As long as I decide that it's not going to be their business, I will use every foible to keep them guessing. So some people think I'm not married, some think I'm divorced, some think the librarian and I have something going. They're pretty much confused. People at school don't know much about me and I've been teaching for over 24 years. My kids have no earthly idea where I live. Sometimes I tell them I live at the beach and sometimes I tell them I live in another county. Once I even said I commuted from Georgia.

More than half of the participants are or were in relationships lasting 10 years or more. All said that no one at their schools knew about their partners. They all agreed that it would be most unusual to not know about a colleague's heterosexual husband or wife, yet they did not dare share such information about themselves with their colleagues, supervisors, or students. These individuals are pretending and hiding as a means to protect their public image. One teacher shared an event that occurred because his colleagues thought he was single:

I was considered to be the only single person on a project and got elected to do all the evening work. When I complained about it, they said, "But you're single." I said, "That has absolutely nothing to do with it." I won that battle, but I kept thinking, "I am not single and this is putting a strain on my relationship." We walk around pretending to be single. It's really difficult.

One teacher with whom I met late one afternoon described an experience that had occurred earlier that day. She reported, as in the previous example, that colleagues believe she is single. She was angered at not being able to take her partner of 12 years to a party at her principal's house. She explained:

I went to a function today at my principal's house. My partner would have loved to go. Everyone brought their spouses. There's no way I'd take the chance. A part of me feels cheated. I wish I had the same privilege to treat [my partner] like everyone else gets to treat their spouse.

Several teachers commented on their vulnerability based on being older and having taught for some time. One veteran teacher commented:

I'm much more concerned now about anyone finding out I'm a lesbian than I was when I was a younger teacher. I'm older now. I have more to lose. I have more concerns now because I don't want to lose my job or get transferred. It seems that the older people get and the more comfortable we get, the more scared and closeted we become. We'll lose it all.

The fear of discovery of their homosexual orientation caused some teachers to reconsider their vocation. One teacher expressed great frustration at having to live with such fear and with hiding his sexual identity. He was one of several participants in this study who was considering leaving the teaching profession in northeast Florida because of the intense difficulty of hiding.

To be honest with you, I've been working on my resume and sending it out. I'm to the point where I want to teach somewhere where I can feel safe and be honest about who I am. I hate not being able to be truthful with everyone. It gets too difficult to figure out who you've told what, when and how, and I don't want to have to mess with it. It's so difficult to be one way here [at home] and another way at school.

Distancing oneself from issues of homosexuality was the third identity management strategy described by Woods and Harbeck (1992). Participants in this study, as in the work by Woods and Harbeck, worried that if they intervened in situations at their schools, their own sexual identity would be revealed. Teachers in this study reported that they usually remain silent when hearing homophobic comments. They also reported that they feel powerless to assist gay or lesbian students or to provide education and information about sexual orientation issues or topics considered taboo, such as information about HIV-related issues.

By employing these strategies, participants acknowledged that they were not acting as role models, nor were they providing accurate information needed by their students. None discussed how these strategies might covertly communicate the same messages to their students that they reportedly received when they were young—that being gay or lesbian was a thing to hide and must not be acknowledged or discussed. Once again the overriding issue was fear of discovery and job loss.

This fear of discovery was evidenced when participants were asked to sign the required consent form to participate in this study. Each had the option of signing her or his actual name, using a pseudonym, or using an X to signify that she or he read and understood the parameters of consent. Every participant in this study selected the X option. Historically, the use of the X as a signature denoted one who is not educated or who is somehow unable to sign his or her name. However, these participants used the X for another reason; it validated their intense and dramatic fear of discovery. Even though a pseudonym would have provided the same level of anonymity, the selection of the X option may have reflected the deep fear of exposure felt by these educators.

Summary. The participants in this study often related that it is extremely unsafe to share information about their sexual orientation or their personal lives for fear of harassment, rejection, or job loss. They repeatedly expressed great frustration about this insecurity and about their perception of their extreme vulnerability. As a result, the filter of fear is highly dominant in their lives and integral to the interpretive model used in this study.

The Silence

Lesbian writer Adrienne Rich (1986) described the feeling of invisibility by saying it was like looking into a mirror and seeing nothing. That sense of non-being is a phenomenon which, for many gays and lesbians, begins at the moment when they are aware of difference and when they simultaneously discover the need for silence about their sexual orientation. This silence compounds the situation because it adds its own consequences of invisibility to lesbian and gay oppression.

The gay and lesbian educators in northeast Florida who participated in this study discussed a conscious decision to remain silent about their sexual orientation rather than risk harassment, rejection, and job termination. The previous section presented several participants who reported elaborate efforts to appear heterosexual, one response to the need to be silent about their sexual orientation. These teachers linked their vulnerability to local prejudices and hostilities that they stated were ever present.

Because communities have overtly demanded that lesbian and gay educators remain silent about their homosexuality, these educators constructed walls of resistance. Silence became the only thing that felt safe. "This silence is like a cultural mask behind which no one must speak openly about homosexuality" (Wishik & Pierce, 1995, 51). Kissen (1996a) noted an irony here; such self-protection requires intense energy that could be focused on teaching and learning. The energy teachers spend hiding and being hyper-vigilant drained their time, their skills, and their minds.

Although none of the participants described themselves as feeling shamed, each seem to be struggling with that underlying emotion. Unfortunately, silence reinforces shame (Kaufman & Raphael, 1996; Sedgewick, 1990). "What cannot be openly expressed is perceived as too shameful to speak about. It is shame that bars the tongue from speaking" (Kaufman & Raphael, 1996, 10). When people are neither able nor allowed to speak openly, they experience an intense sense of shame about who they are. When institutions such as public school systems, universities, and state legislatures impose shame, as it is perceived in Florida and northeast Florida, it becomes a powerful form of oppression (Kaufman & Raphael, 1996).

Not one person in this study was open in the public school system about her or his sexual orientation. All formed lives in the workplace based on the conspiracy of silence. Participants described three areas relating to the silence: how they felt about being silent; how they were affected by being silent; and how they were not able to speak up and speak out for their students as well as for themselves. One teacher described her feelings about having to be silent, as well as the energy she must daily give to reinforcing that silence:

I've heard a lot of comments, not really about me personally, but about lesbians and gays that tell me that I need to be quiet about it. I learned to be silent in the school system through my own common sense and on the advice of other gay and lesbian teachers. But being silent affects my relationships with my coworkers, my principal, and the parents. I feel that I can never share an experience that I've been through with my partner, however appropriate it might be.

My social activity with my peers is very limited because I can't bring my partner along or discuss our life. And it always comes back to that fear—what if somebody finds out? So I pretty much live with a low-grade fear every day, which I feel is detrimental to my entire being. I feel like I'm missing out on a lot. The silence means we spend our whole lives lying. We live our lives in such paranoid fashion, petrified that anybody would find out.

Participants spoke about the fear of discovery throughout this research. It was both their underlying and their overriding emotion. Another participant shared both how that fear constructed her life and informed her behavior in her school, and how the fear led to silence and loneliness:

My partner and I teach at the same school. We're not out. I don't really know what out is, but we're not out. We go to school every day with a fear that someone will discover the truth about us. I've never felt any compulsion to tell anybody, primarily because I don't trust anybody. The longer I'm there, the people you think you can trust, for various and sundry reasons, just are not. Sure, you feel like reaching out, but you don't for your own safety's sake. It just means keeping my private life private, and that's the way it is. It gets lonesome sometimes. There's nobody I'm close to. I don't enjoy it. It does bother me. It's a lonely way to live. And the assumptions they make about me I can't correct or agree with. That is the biggest lie of all. That's the biggest lie of all.

Summary. There is, then, in addition, widespread lying among these educators; the lying contributes to growing resentment towards colleagues, the school system, and the community. The participants reported that their silence about who they are is extraordinarily painful and that it exerts tremendous power over them. It seems that their fear—the filter of fear in the model—forces them to remain silent.

Suggestions for Changes

hooks and West (1991, 95) spoke of struggle and change in the Black community, but their words are applicable to other minorities and to lesbian and gay educators in particular.

The crucial issue is what are we going to do now? Not how are we going to look, or what political slogan are we going to wear, but what forms of substantive struggle are we going to engage with our minds and bodies? I think there is real loss of a sense of what to do. To be a people without an immediate sense of direction aggravates already present feelings of powerlessness.

This community of lesbian and gay educators appeared to lack knowledge of what to do for themselves, for their students, and for the educational system. They all described a sense of powerlessness that prevents them from pursuing their teaching goals and from reaching out to their students.

Participants explored the topic of what changes they would make in the public school system in order to create a safe and welcoming environment for all teachers and students. Because state and local policies affect the personal lives of these participants, they talked about the nature of that influence. By presenting their suggestions for change, participants became involved in and excited at the prospect of having a sense of control in what they perceive to be a powerless situation. Their suggestions provided validation for them and expanded and enriched the literature.

The participants' suggestions for change echoed the spirit of the literature, which itself calls for change. These suggestions included the following: curriculum expansion in teacher education and recertification courses; in-service education for teachers, counselors, and school administrators about sexual orientation issues in education; provision of benefits for domestic partners; and a mechanism for professional and collegial support of teachers as well as for students. The most frequently mentioned suggestion concerned job protection. In one teacher's words:

Well, first of all, the anti-discrimination legislation needs to be passed so I'd have something to fight back with. To know that they can't fire you on this. It would be nice to have job protection, and I could be free to be myself.

Another suggestion was for lesbian and gay teachers be open about their sexual orientation. The participants said most people would change their attitudes if they had the opportunity to know individuals who are gay or lesbian. However, these teachers reinforced their position that they were unable to be open about their sexual orientation and to provide that opportunity; at the same time, they repeated that being open would change the educational environment. This was another example of the conflict these educators verbally experience. One teacher shared her opinion:

Teachers and counselors don't know. They need to meet gay people. They need to know what it's like to be a gay person. I'm sure most of them don't even know any. I'm sure they'd act differently if they did.

Another suggestion was education and training in a variety of arenas. Several teachers said in-service education experiences that focused on sexual orientation issues or college-level courses taught as part of the teacher education or recertification curriculum would be helpful. However, they had reservations about the in-service process because, in their opinion, teachers generally dislike in-service programs immensely. One teacher described a general feeling about in-service education:

Speaking from years of experience, most teachers are turned off by in-service of any kind, and we've had some really bad in-services. Having in-services, well, there's never a good time for an in-service, and people generally don't go to them unless they're required.

The participants suggested that discussion of sexual orientation issues be included in teacher education programs and in multicultural courses for teachers at all local universities and community colleges. A recent graduate said:

There's a big push for multicultural education, and I think that being gay or lesbian is certainly multicultural. It should be included. It's not just a matter of race. At this point, the multicultural classes are pretty much mandatory at UNF [the University of North Florida]. We should be included. That would be a start. Education is needed to change the process. You've got to educate the parents. You've got to educate the teachers. You've got to educate everyone.

Another suggestion concerned the public school libraries. Books about lesbian and gay people, history, and issues should be in school libraries. Participants acknowledged that the politically right-wing's current efforts at censorship would make it difficult to get these books into the libraries of the northeast Florida public schools. One teacher offered a suggestion:

I want to see gay-positive books in the library, but you can't even get Judy Blume books in the library. But *Annie on My Mind* and other books for teens, *Confessions of a Rock Lobster*, *One Teenager in Ten*, are excellent for teens about being gay.

Summary. All the participants reported a belief that implementing these suggestions would be necessary for change to occur, but none revealed a willingness or acknowledged an ability to initiate the changes. Although they agreed that change needs to take place, they did not state how to make change happen. The suggestions they offered required undefined action by others. Although participants considered their problems and made suggestions to alleviate them, nearly all returned to the idea that others must make the changes and that they themselves were powerless to do so. As portrayed in the dynamics of the model, these silent lesbian

and gay educators stated that they feel unable to be change agents because they allow their workplace contacts—students, parents of students,
colleagues, supervisors, and even the community-at-large—to have ultimate power to determine their continued employment in the public
school system.

Chapter 6

Creating Change: Envisioning the Future

Sears (1991, 433) noted that the test of qualitative inquiry is to illuminate "the lives of a few well chosen individuals." This research study focused on 16 lesbian and gay educators in northeast Florida who offered their voices to describe their lives in the present, their experiences from the past, and their suggestions for the future. The analysis and interpretation of the data, using a model developed from a basis in the literature, showed a pattern of difficulties faced by gay and lesbian teachers. These teachers reported that, because of these difficulties, they engage in behaviors that they identify as restricting their ability for complete participation in the educational process.

These gay and lesbian educators offered portraits of an educational setting that they perceive to be unsafe and devaluing. To them it imposes isolation, reinforces their silence, inhibits their teaching potential, and suppresses the full expression of their teaching vocation. Their stories are not all-inclusive, but the illumination of their experiences provides new insight and information about a population of teachers in northeast Florida.

Illness, death, painful memories, and a sense of hopelessness permeated some of the interviews. Some participants acknowledged, with ironic humor, the absurdity of the silence, the discrimination, and the inability to have one's partner's photograph on a desk at school. But nearly all 16 teachers in this study stated that they would like to be open and honest about their sexual orientation; that they desire to be available as role models, mentors, and advocates for homosexual and heterosexual students alike; that they would like to do their work without fear of harassment, humiliation, or pressure to resign. They want to teach without the fear of losing their jobs. All 16 teachers believe discrimination based on sexual orientation is widespread and deeply ingrained in their districts in northeast Florida. All of the participants described northeast Florida as an intolerant, conservative region, whose primary political and social influences are the Southern Baptist Church and the Northeast Florida Christian Coalition. Some of the participants attended churches or synagogues regularly; however, nearly all expressed anger toward organized religion, exacerbated by the omnipresence of and the attitudes expressed about gays and lesbians by the Southern Baptist churches and the Christian Coalition. Nonetheless, they individually find ways to teach despite the prejudice and discrimination they perceive, observe, or experience in the public schools. They reported that their invisibility is personally very costly in terms of decreased self-esteem and increased loneliness and fear. The fear that students, colleagues, and supervisors would discover their sexual orientation permeated every interview.

Participants frequently discussed their isolation from students, colleagues, and administrators, as well as from the gay community. They described the larger lesbian and gay community as fragmented and lacking in support and camaraderie. This lack of participation contrasted with what Ross, Fernandez-Esquer, and Seibt (1996, 423) noted—that the lesbian and gay community can "function in the sense of a social support mechanism for those who identify as gay and who have access to other members of this community." Even though, as these authors noted, social support systems may buffer stress and offer protection against discrimination, rejection, and marginalization, few participants in this study neither identified with nor participated in a meaningful way with the gay community in northeast Florida. They shared that they experienced little ordinary social support, a condition that may lead to a sense of helplessness when crises occur.

Participants reported that while a significant number of lesbian and gay teachers and administrators live in northeast Florida, methods for organization, support, and communication do not exist among them. All cited fear of discovery and subsequent job loss as the reasons for not developing a support network. By their silence with one another, therefore, an implicit rule of limited communication emerged. The participants described communication of information among lesbian and gay teachers as occurring primarily through hearsay and observational reports. Third parties also communicated some information that was later shared. Accounts of real or imagined events were the means used to transmit information and to suggest attitudes, with intuition guiding the translation of messages into subsequent behavior.

These educators verbalized high levels of self-imposed isolation and stress. They expressed no confidence that colleagues would support and protect them if other colleagues became aware of their sexual orientation. Indeed, their overriding fear throughout this research was the potential loss of jobs if their sexual orientation was discovered. All reported compartmentalizing their vocation from their sexual orientation, a strategy which kept their work and personal lives separate and disconnected; they assumed that such compartmentalization was both foreign to and unnecessary for their heterosexual colleagues.

These educators also reported that in their schools they were frequently dishonest about their lives, a practice that often resulted in a growing resentment towards colleagues, the school system, and the community. They noted both a fear of administrators and a lack of support from supervisors. They did not trust colleagues enough to form friendships or on-the-job support systems. As a result, there was a self-imposed alienation from colleagues and administrators reported by nearly all the participants. The alienation even extended to the point that none of the participants could clearly describe what would constitute support for lesbian and gay teachers.

None of these teachers perceived the parents of their students to be allies. Indeed, they described parents as having the power to remove teachers from their jobs. Ever present was a fear of accusations of child molestation. Each teacher described efforts to prevent the possibility of such charges, efforts that also sacrificed the opportunity for closeness with their students. They described the extremes to which they went to ensure career safety, often at the cost of the human warmth and expression of caring that are traditionally associated with teachers.

Even though these teachers also reported numerous examples of discrimination, harassment, and policy violation in some of the public schools in northeast Florida, they reported that for the most part they chose to remain silent. For example, when homophobic comments were heard within their public school settings, the teachers reported that they often had to decide between personal protection and the confrontation of discriminatory practices. Their decisions typically did not include proactive efforts to protect themselves or their students from attack and rejection. They knew they were neither acting as role models nor providing support needed by their students. All stated that they would like to acknowledge lesbian and gay students and assist them as needed, but they said they were not willing to be advocates for these students for fear of discovery of their own sexual orientation and subsequent job loss. They reported that, unlike their heterosexual colleagues, they did not share information about their personal lives with students; thus separateness from students was a common experience. They repeatedly expressed their extreme vulnerability and the frustration that comes from being unable to act

All described gay and lesbian adolescents as an at-risk population in northeast Florida that needs acknowledgment and assistance. Although these teachers reported occasional efforts to provide information about sexual orientation issues to their students, they also reported that school board policies in northeast Florida and their own limited knowledge of the history of gay and lesbian culture restrict them from providing much information to their students. Their silence was extraordinarily powerful since it extended beyond themselves and affected their concerns for student welfare.

The results of this study are remarkable in that the participants' perceptions and fears as lesbian and gay teachers sounded so similar to one another, despite their ordinary life differences and separate situations. The fear of job loss was consistently in the forefront of each participant's concerns. This group of lesbian and gay educators lacked an understanding of what to do to improve conditions; they all described an immense sense of powerlessness. All reported that change was necessary, but no one felt safe enough or empowered enough to suggest such change openly or to pursue change actively.

THE POSSIBILITIES

Both physical and psychological safety and inclusion are critical if teachers are to discharge their duties effectively. The interview data and the literature suggest policy changes that might ensure safety, freedom from discrimination, and equal opportunity for all educators and students. Beyond policy changes, educators themselves might initiate changes within education and training programs designed for both new and continuing teachers. They might create and enhance support systems and organizations for gay and lesbian teachers as well as for students. Further, with the development of curriculum and library collections about lesbian and gay issues, history, and people, students in the schools would be able to expand their own knowledge base.

At the State Level

Legal initiatives directed toward change are appropriate at the state level. The *Florida Civil Rights Act* and the *Florida State Employment Policy* (Florida Statutes, 1995e, 1995f) must be amended to include the words *sexual orientation*. With the current absence of such terminology,

Florida law offers no employment protection for gay or lesbian people. Such amendments would prohibit employers from terminating workers or otherwise discriminating against people in Florida, including educators, on the basis of sexual orientation.

The *Code of Ethics and the Principles of Professional Conduct of the Education Profession in Florida* (Florida Statutes, 1995a, b) must include *sexual orientation* in every section where lists of characteristics are identified. Further, regardless of length of service, the brochure with these statements must be distributed to all teachers. Penalties identified in the brochure must be enforced for all violations.

Finally, a "Dignity for All Students Act," similar to that pending in California and New York, must focus on the roles of teachers and administrators in preventing anti-gay harassment. It should mandate training for all school personnel on the effects of anti-gay harassment on students and teachers, how to spot and stop such harassment, and require schools to devise ways of dealing with students who bully those they think may be gay. It would also require guidelines for appropriate responses to anti-gay harassment, as well as the designation of a person in each school to work with students who are victims of anti-gay harassment (Boerner, 1999).

At the School Board Level

The participants, as well as the literature, suggested that to ensure job security and safety at the local level, school boards must take the lead in providing a climate that is free from discrimination. Such action might take several forms: the development of an explicit policy that prohibits harassment, name calling, and verbal and physical abuse of all school personnel regardless of sexual orientation; the development of methods for reporting inappropriate and harmful behavior as described by the *Florida Hate Crimes Act* (Florida Statutes, 1995i); and the identification of an advocate or ombudsperson who would address sexual orientation issues in each district to ensure the availability of a professionally trained person as a mediator and informed spokesperson for all members of the school community.

At the Level of School and Educational Leaders

Superintendents, district administrators, principals, and other educational leaders in the community are responsible for creating a work environment that is free from discrimination and that supports and encourages teachers in their efforts with students. Participants in the study offered educational leaders suggestions for developing such an environment: the denunciation by educational leaders of homophobia and other forms of oppression, accompanied by leaders' efforts to be role models, allies, and agents of change; the replacement of myths and stereotypes with facts about gays and lesbians; the development of experiences to improve intergroup relations; the development of plans for conflict resolution in situations where sexual orientation issues play a role; the development and sponsorship of mandated training for school personnel about gay and lesbian adolescents and the issues they face; and a requirement that parents who complain about sexual orientation issues or lesbian and gay personnel do so in writing specifically stating their objections and the reasons behind them. Such changes would validate the commitment by educational leaders that intolerance is not acceptable in the public school culture of northeast Florida.

School leaders must also pursue the inclusion of the issues of gay and lesbian students in prevention programs designed for at-risk students, such as dropout prevention programs, suicide prevention programs, health programs, and programs designed to reduce teen pregnancy. Also appropriate would be support for teachers and other educators who wish to pursue their own professional development at conferences and through educational materials focused on sexual orientation issues.

At the Level of the Students

The participants and the literature suggest what must be done to assist gay and lesbian students. These students need to be informed that teachers are prohibited from discrimination against or harassment of students based on sexual orientation, and that recourse is available if such behavior occurs. Students must receive information about the mechanisms by which to report harassment and discrimination without trepidation. Indeed, school personnel should encourage students to report such harassment to teachers, principals, counselors, parents, or other trusted adults, whether the student experienced the harassment personally or observed it. Educators might also assist gay and lesbian students in establishing Gay/Straight Alliances (GSAs) in the schools, with the assurance that these organizations will be as supported by the school, as are other student groups. Assistance in establishing a GSA may be obtained through the Gay Lesbian Straight Educators Network (GLSEN) national offices.

Lesbian and gay students must be included actively in the total school culture. Creating a climate of inclusion may take several forms: having gay-sensitive and age-appropriate materials in the libraries to which students have access; displaying pictures or posters of lesbian and gay individuals and gay-related events when appropriate, such as during National Lesbian and Gay History month each October; making available gay-related materials, magazines, and flyers in the offices of counselors, coaches, and school health nurses, positioned in ways that allow students to obtain them without notice; and providing information for students and their parents about resources in the northeast Florida area, including the Jacksonville Area Sexual Minority Youth Network (JASMYN) and Parents and Friends of Lesbians and Gays (PFLAG).

At the Level of the Faculty and Staff

Faculty and staff can ensure a safe, secure, and inclusive environment. When teachers acknowledge the contributions of gay and lesbian people within the curriculum and when they replace myths and stereotypes with accurate information about lesbians and gay men, they actively promote an inclusive school environment which respects all members. Teachers' familiarity with local resources would enable them to refer lesbian and gay students and their families to appropriate information and services. Teachers themselves must also enforce the rules that prohibit homophobic and discriminatory language, and file complaints when other teachers or administrators make derogatory statements. Even more assertively and as a means to accomplish such unified purposes, educators might form networks of both gay and non-gay teachers modeled by GLSEN.

At the Level of the Parents of Students

Parents of gay and non-gay students are politically powerful and have a personal stake in their children's healthy future. Parents of any student, but especially those of lesbian or gay students, could attend meetings of support groups such as Parents and Friends of Lesbians and Gays (PFLAG) in order to gain more information about gay and lesbian families and to receive support from others who may be more comfortable and familiar with the issue areas. If parents believe their child is experiencing discrimination, harassment, or abuse because of sexual orientation issues at school, they need to file a complaint with school personnel and the police. Parents of gay and non-gay students alike could also interview school board members and candidates to ensure that the safety and educational needs of all children, including lesbian and gay children, are met.

Educational Leadership in Northeast Florida

According to the participants, many teachers in northeast Florida receive their college education locally, either at the Florida Community College at Jacksonville, the University of North Florida, or Jacksonville University. Many pursue their teacher recertification locally as well. The participants suggested that these institutions offer courses or integrate sexual orientation issues into existing courses for all majors, especially majors in education. These institutions must also vigilantly make and keep their environments safe for lesbian and gay students, faculty, and staff, regardless of the local culture of discrimination. They also suggested that conferences, seminars, and workshops be hosted by these educational institutions which address sexual orientation issues in schools.

RECOMMENDATIONS FOR FURTHER RESEARCH

Analysis of the data collected during the course of this study pointed to additional areas appropriate for research. Because fear was such a central construct in these teachers' discussions, in-depth exploration of the basis for the fear and the complexity of its dynamics are needed. Investigation of the effects of the lesbian or gay educator's professional life on personal interactions with domestic partners would also be appropriate. It would be appropriate as well to explore the knowledge, beliefs, behavior, and attitudes of lesbian and gay educators as those factors affect their professional and personal lives. Additionally, research could explore the professional and social interactions of gay and lesbian teachers with colleagues as well as with students.

Future research might also include exploration of the life-satisfaction issues of gay and lesbian teachers related to their interactions with and in the larger gay and lesbian community. Further questions arise, as well, regarding aspects of sexual identity development, identity management, and the development of personal support systems of gay and lesbian teachers in northeast Florida.

An additional area for further research would be a comparison of lesbian and gay people in education with lesbian and gay people in other employment areas in the same geographic region to determine if similar experiences of fear and isolation exist. A comparison of the lesbian or gay classroom teacher with the gay or lesbian administrator would be useful in learning if there are differences in experiences across the educational hierarchy. It would also be useful to examine the perspectives of school principals and other administrators toward gay and lesbian educators and about gay and lesbian issues in terms of levels of awareness, sensitivity, and understanding. Because the field of lesbian and gay studies and research is quite new, many possibilities exist for research and scholarship.

CONCLUSION

Through the voices and experiences of the lesbian and gay public school teachers interviewed in this study, an interpretation of their worlds was presented. These educators may have the same everyday professional encounters as their heterosexual colleagues, but there is a significance difference: They enter their classrooms and interact with students and colleagues daily with the overwhelming fear that their sexual orientation will be discovered and ultimately they will be terminated from employment. These educators became teachers with the same hopes and expectations of wanting to assist students to learn and grow, and they continue to do their work despite the difficulties they encounter by being silent about who they really are. Some of them remain in the teaching profession in northeast Florida in spite of those difficulties, and some leave to seek safer employment environments.

It will take overt political, social, and legal action and courageous educational leadership by individuals and groups in northeast Florida to change the current environment in which lesbian and gay educators frequently live silently under sanctioned discrimination. All teachers and students have a right to work and learn in a safe environment that is free from discrimination and harassment, and that welcomes the full participation of every person, regardless of sexual orientation.

Resources and Recommended Reading

WEBSITES

Gay Lesbian Straight Educators Network (GLSEN)
http://www.glsen.org
(212) 727-013

National Consortium of Directors of LGBT Resources in Higher Education
http://www.uic.edu/orgs/lgbt
(310) 206-3628

Parents and Friends of Lesbians and Gays (PFLAG)
http://www.pflag.org
(202) 638-4200

RECOMMENDED READING

Blumenfeld, W. *Homophobia: How We All Pay the Price.* 1992. Beacon Press.
Harbeck, K. (Ed.). *Coming Out of the Classroom Closet: Gay and Lesbian Students, Teachers, and Curricula.* 1992. Haworth Publications.
Jennings, K. *One Teacher in 10: Gay and Lesbian Educators Tell Their Stories.* 1994. Alyson Publications.
Kissen, R. M. *The Last Closet: The Real Lives of Lesbian and Gay Teachers.* 1996. Heinemann Press.
Nabozny v. *Podlesny,* No. 95-3634, 1996 WL 4208031, *affd.,* U.S. Court of Appeals, (7th Cir. Wis.).
National Education Association. *Affording Equal Opportunity to Gay and Lesbian Students through Teaching and Counseling: A Training Handbook for Educators.* 1991.

Sanlo, R. (Ed.). *Working with Lesbian, Gay, Bisexual, and Transgender College Students: A Handbook for Faculty and Administrators.* 1998. Greenwood Press.

Sears, J. T. *Growing Up Gay in the South: Race, Gender, and Journeys of the Spirit.* 1991. Haworth Press.

Walling, D. (Ed.). *Open Lives, Safe Schools.* 1996. Phi Delta Kappa Educational Foundation.

References

ACLU News. (July 28, 1997). *Same-sex marriage ban approval in Florida.* www.aclu.org/news/N072897a.html.

————. (July 28, 1997). *Judge upholds Florida's ban on lesbian and gay adoptions.* www.aclu.org/news/N072897a.html

————. (May 14, 1999). Federal Appeals Court rules unconstitutional religious exercises in public schools. www.aclu.org/news/W060297a.html.

Altenbaugh, R. (Ed.). (1992). *The teacher's voice: A social history of teaching in 20th century America.* Washington, DC: Falmer.

Barale, M. (1989). The lesbian academic: Negotiating new boundaries. In E. Rothblum & E. Cole (Eds.), *Loving boldly: Issues facing lesbians* (pp. 183–194). New York: Harrington Park.

Beake, J. (1998, Oct. 20). Castor seeks redress for discrimination. *Oracle, 36* (40). 1, 14. University of South Florida.

Beauchamp, G. A. (1968). *Curriculum theory.* Wilmette, IL: The Kagg Press.

Berzon, B. (1992). *Positively gay: New approaches to gay and lesbian life.* Berkeley, CA: Celestial Arts.

Blumenfeld, W. (Ed.). (1992). *Homophobia: How we all pay the price.* Boston: Beacon.

Bogden, R., & Biklen, S. (1992). *Qualitative research for education: An introduction to theory and methods.* (2nd ed.). Boston: Allyn & Bacon.

Boswell, J. (1980). *Christianity, social tolerance, and homosexuality: Gay people in western Europe from the beginning of the Christian era to the fourteenth century.* Chicago: University of Chicago.

Boxall, B., & Noriyuki, D. (1999, May 28). *Abuse of gay students brings increase in lawsuits.* Los Angeles Times, A1. www.latimes.com.

ChannelQ Newsdesk. (1998, March 4). *Children's book kept out of library.* newsdesk@channelq.com.

Charisse, M. (1996). *Radio station kills chorus spot in dispute over the "G" word*. Folio Weekly. Jacksonville, FL. mcharisse@aol.com.

Croteau, J. M., & Lark, J. S. (1995). On being lesbian, gay, or bisexual in student affairs: A national survey of experiences on the job. *National Association of Student Personnel Administrators Journal, 32* (3), pp. 189–197.

Donnelly, F. (1992, March 27). Homosexuality taken out of Stanton paper. *Florida Times-Union.* 1, 3.

Donovan, F. (1938). *The school ma'am.* New York: Frederick A. Stokes.

Dressler, J. (1985). Survey of school principals regarding alleged homosexual teachers in the classroom: How likely (really) is discharge? *University of Dayton Law Review, 10* (3), pp. 599–620.

Duberman, M. (1991). *About time: Exploring the gay past.* New York: Meridian.

Eichelberger, R. (1989). *Disciplined inquiry: Understanding and doing educational research.* White Plains, NY: Longman.

Eisner, E. W. (1991). *The enlightened eye: Qualitative inquiry and the enhancement of educational practice.* New York: Macmillan.

Fine, M. (1989). Silencing and nurturing voice in an improbable context: Urban adolescents in pubic schools. In H. A. Giroux & P. McLaren (Eds.), *Critical pedagogy, the state, and cultural struggle* (pp. 152–173). Albany, NY: State University of New York Press.

Finnegan, D. G., & McNally, E. B. (1987). *Dual identities: Counseling chemically dependent gay men and lesbians.* Center City, MN: Hazelden.

First Amendment Center (1997, Oct. 22). *Lesbian teacher sues over school district's gag order.* http://www.fac.org.

Fischer, E. (1994). *Aimee and Jaguar: A love story, Berlin 1943.* N.Y.: Harper-Collins Publications.

Florida Legislative Investigative Committee. (1964). *Homosexuality and citizenship in Florida: A report of the Florida Legislative Investigation Committee.* Tallahassee, FL.

Florida Statutes. (1981). Chapter 81-206—*Specific appropriations*, Sec. 237, *Operating capital outlay.*

———. (1995a). Chapter 6B-1.001—*Code of ethics of the education profession in Florida.*

———. (1995b). Chapter 6B-1.006—*Principles of professional conduct for the education profession in Florida.*

———. (1995c). Chapter 6B-4(6)—*Florida State Board of Education administrative rules: Criteria for suspension and dismissal, moral turpitude.*

———. (1995d). Chapter 63:04—*Florida Adoption Act*, 63.042 (3).

———. (1995e). Chapter 110—*Employment policy of the state*, 110.105 (2).

———. (1995f). Chapter 760—*Discrimination in the treatment of persons, Part I, Florida Civil Rights Act of 1992*, 760.01–760.11 (1).

———. (1995g). Chapter 775—*Florida Criminal Code*, 775.085, *Evidencing prejudice while committing offense; enhanced penalties*, 775.085 (1).

———. (1995h). Chapter 847—*Obscene literature; profanity.*

———. (1995i). Chapter 877.19(b)—*Hate Crimes Reporting Act.*

————. (1995j). Chapter 233.0672—*Health education; Instruction in acquired immune deficiency syndrome.*

Florida Supreme Court. (Feb. 1982). *Department of Education, State Board of Education, Turlington & D'Alemberte* v. *Lewis & Firestone,* No. 61,241.

Fried, B., Ferejohn, J., Franklin, J., Greely. H., Kelman, M., Meier, J., Satz, D., & Sharigan, K. (1994). *Domestic partner benefits: A case study.* Washington, DC: College and University Personnel Association.

Friedman, R. C., & Downey, J. I. (1994). Homosexuality. *The New England Journal of Medicine, 331* (14), pp. 923–930.

Geertz, C. (1973). *The interpretation of cultures.* New York: Basic Books.

Gibson, P. (1989). Gay male and lesbian youth suicide. In M. Feinleib (Ed.), *Report of the Secretary's Task Force on Youth Suicide, 3.* U.S. Department of Health and Human Services, National Institute of Mental Health, 3-110-3-143.

Giroux, H. (1992). *Border crossings: Cultural workers and the politics of education.* New York: Routledge, Chapman, and Hall.

Glionna, J. (1998, Dec. 30). Gay teacher fights defections from his classes. *Los Angeles Times.* A1, A3.

Gold, S. (1999, Jan. 15). Universities' bias rule unchanged. *South Florida Sun-Sentinel.* http://www.sun-sentinel.com.

Grayson, D. A. (1987, Summer). Emerging equity issues related to homosexuality in education. *Peabody Journal of Education, 64,* pp. 132–45.

Griffin, P. (1992a). From hiding out to coming out: Empowering lesbian and gay educators. In K. Harbeck (Ed.), *Coming out of the classroom closet: Gay and lesbian students, teachers, and curricula* (pp. 167–196). New York: Haworth.

————. (1992b). Lesbian and gay educators: Opening the classroom closet. In J. Sears (Ed.), *Empathy, 3* (1), pp. 25–28.

Harbeck, K. (Ed.). (1992a). *Coming out of the classroom closet: Gay and lesbian students, teachers, and curricula.* New York: Haworth.

————. (1992b). Gay and lesbian educators: Past history/future prospects. In K. Harbeck (Ed.), *Coming out of the classroom closet: Gay and lesbian students, teachers, and curricula* (pp. 121–140). New York: Haworth.

————. (1995). Invisible no more: Addressing the needs of lesbian, gay, bisexual youth and their advocates. In G. Unks (Ed.), *The gay teen: Educational practice and theory for lesbian, gay, and bisexual adolescents* (pp. 125–134). New York: Routledge.

————. (1997). *Gay and lesbian educators: Personal freedoms, public constraints.* Malden, MA: Amethyst Press.

Harvard Law Review. (1990). *Sexual orientation and the law.* Cambridge, MA: Harvard University Press.

Heger, H. (1980). *The men with the pink triangle.* Boston: Alyson Publications.

Herek, G. (1989). Hate crimes against lesbians and gay men. *American Psychologist, 44,* pp. 948–955.

Heshusius, L. (1994). Freeing ourselves from objectivity: Managing subjectivity or turning toward a participatory mode of consciousness? *Educational Researcher, 23* (3), pp. 15–22.

hooks, b., & West, C. (1991). *Breaking bread: Insurgent Black intellectual life.* Boston, MA: South End Press.

Human Rights Campaign. (1998, June 11). *Southern Baptist Convention continues issuing bizarre anti-gay resolutions.* Press release. Washington, DC. www.hrc.org.

Jacksonville Chamber of Commerce. (1999). Jacksonville, FL: www.jackchamber.org/community_index.htm.

Jennings, K. (Ed.). (1994). *One teacher in 10: Gay and lesbian educators tell their stories.* Boston: Alyson Publications.

Jersild, A. (1955). *When teachers face themselves.* New York: Columbia University Teachers College Press.

Journal of the Senate. (1977a, April 13). Florida Legislature. Pp. 145–146. Tallahassee, FL.

———. (1977b, May 11). Florida Legislature. Pp. 371–372. Tallahassee, FL.

Juul, T. P., & Repa, T. (1993). *A survey to examine the relationship of the openness of self-identified lesbian, gay male, and bisexual public school teachers to job stress and job satisfaction.* Paper presented at the meeting of the American Educational Research Association, Atlanta, GA.

Katz, J. (1976). *Gay American history: Lesbians and gay men in the U.S.A.* New York: Thomas Y. Crowell.

Katz, M. S. (1998). *APA rebukes Rep. Dempsey.* APA Release #98.56. email communication. mkatz@psych.org.

Kaufman, G., & Raphael, L. (1996). *Coming out of shame: Transforming gay and lesbian lives.* New York: Doubleday.

Khayatt, M. (1992). *Lesbian teachers: An invisible presence.* Albany, NY: State University of New York.

Kindred, L. W., Bagin, D., & Gallagher, D. R. (1990). *The school and community relations.* (4th ed.). Needham Heights, MA: Alyn and Bacon.

Kissen, R. M. (1996a). *The last closet: The real lives of lesbian and gay teachers.* Portsmouth, NH: Heinemann.

———. (1996b). Teaching under siege: Lesbian and gay educators in Colorado and Oregon. In D. Walling (Ed.), *Open lives, safe schools* (pp. 223–236). Bloomington, IN: Phi Delta Kappa Educational Foundation.

Krysiak, G. (1987). Very silent and gay minority. *School Counselor, 34* (4), pp. 304–307.

Lauritsen J., & Thorstad, D. (1974). *The early homosexual rights movement (1864–1935).* New York: Times Change Press.

Lee, R. M. (1993). *Doing research on sensitive topics.* Newbury Park, CA: Sage.

Lipkin, A. (1995). The case for a gay and lesbian curriculum. In G. Unks (Ed.), *The gay teen: Educational practice and theory for lesbian, gay, and bisexual adolescents* (pp. 31–52). New York: Routledge.

Lortie, D. (1975). *Schoolteacher: A sociological study*. Chicago: University of Chicago.

Marcus, E. (1992). *Making history: The struggle for gay and lesbian equal rights*. New York: HarperCollins.

Marino, T. W. (1995). To be young and gay in America. *Counseling Today, 37* (11), p. 1, 8.

Marshall, C., & Rossman, G. (1995). *Designing qualitative research*. (2nd ed.). Thousand Oaks, CA: Sage Publications.

Mayer, M. (1993). *Gay, lesbian, and heterosexual teachers: An investigation of acceptance of self, acceptance of others, affectional and lifestyle orientation*. New York: Edwin Mellen.

McNaron, T. (1997). *Poisoned ivy: Lesbian and gay academics confronting homophobia*. Philadelphia: Temple University Press.

Merriam, S. (1988). *Case study research in education: A qualitative approach*. San Francisco, CA: Jossey-Bass.

Merton, R. K., Fiske, M. & Kendall, P. L. (1990). *The focused interviews: A manual of problems and procedures*. (2nd ed.). New York: Free Press.

Murphy, J. T. (1980). *Getting the facts: A fieldwork guide for evaluators and policy analysts*. Santa Monica, CA: Goodyear.

Nabozny v. *Podlesny*. No. 95-3634, 1996 WL 4208031, *affd.,* U.S. Court of Appeals, (7th Cir. Wis.).

National Education Association. (1991). *Affording equal opportunity to gay and lesbian students through teaching and counseling: A training handbook for educators*. Washington, DC: National Education Association.

Newman, J. (1990). *America's teachers: An introduction to education*. New York: Longman.

O'Brien, J., & Rohr, E. (1998, Oct. 9). UW student found brutally beaten. *Branding Iron*, p. 1. University of Wyoming.

Olson, M. (1987). A study of gay and lesbian teachers. *Journal of Homosexuality, 13* (4), pp. 73–81.

Pai, Y. (1990). *Cultural foundations of education*. Columbus, OH: Merrill Publishing Co.

Patton, M. Q. (1990). *Qualitative evaluation and research methods*. Newbury Park, CA: Sage.

Pendleton, R. (1993, July 5). The Johns Report identifies teachers. *Florida Times-Union*, p. 1.

Plant, R. (1986). *The pink triangle: The Nazi war against homosexuality*. New York: Henry Holt.

Pollack, R., & Schwartz, C. (1995). *The journey out*. New York: Puffin Books.

Pope, M. (1995). The "salad bowl" is big enough for us all: An argument for the inclusion of lesbians and gay men in any definition of multiculturalism. *Journal of Counseling and Development, 73* (3), pp. 301–304.

Provenzo, E. F. (1990). *Religious fundamentalism and American education: The battle for the public schools*. Albany, NY: State University of New York Press.

Rich, A. (1986). *Blood, bread, and poetry: Selected prose 1979–1985*. New York: Norton.

Ross, M. W., Fernandez-Esquer, M. E., & Seibt, A. (1996). Understanding across the sexual orientation gap: Sexuality as culture. In D. Landis & R. Bhagat (Eds.), (2nd ed.). *Handbook of intercultural training*, pp. 414–430. Thousand Oaks, CA: Sage.

Rubin, H. J., & Rubin, I. S. (1995). *Qualitative interviewing: The art of hearing data*. Thousand Oaks, CA: Sage Publications.

Saunders, J. (1995, July 30). School board near vote on sex education. *The Florida Times-Union*. B1, 2.

Schneider-Vogel, M. (1986). Gay teachers in the classroom: A continuing constitutional debate. *Journal of Law and Education, 15* (3), pp. 285–318.

Schreier, B. (1995). Moving beyond tolerance: A new paradigm for programming about homophobia/biphobia and heterosexism. *Journal of College Student Development, 36* (1), pp. 19–26.

Sciullo, A. (1984). Tolls at the closet doors: A gay history for teachers. (Doctoral dissertation, University of Michigan, Ann Arbor). *Dissertation Abstracts International, 45* (2), p. 497A.

Sears, J. T. (1991). *Growing up gay in the South: Race, gender, and journeys of the spirit*. New York: Haworth.

———. (1992a). *Sexuality and the curriculum*. New York: Teachers College.

———. (1992b). Educators, homosexuality, and homosexual students: Are personal feelings related to professional beliefs? In K. Harbeck (Ed.), *Coming out of the classroom closet: Gay and lesbian students, teachers, and curricula* (pp. 29–80). New York: Haworth.

———. (1995). *The institutional climate for lesbian, gay, and bisexual education faculty: What is the pivotal frame of reference?* Unpublished paper.

———. (1997). *Lonely hunters: An oral history of lesbian and gay southern life, 1948–1968*. Boulder, CO: Westview Press.

Sedgewick, E. (1990). *Epistemology of the closet*. Berkeley, CA: University of California.

Seidman, I. E. (1991). *Interviewing as qualitative research: A guide for researchers in education and the social sciences*. New York: Teachers College Press.

Signorile, M. (1995). *Outing yourself*. New York: Simon & Schuster.

Silin, J. G. (1992). *At the entrance to school: Private lives and professional identities*. Paper presented at the meeting of the American Educational Research Association, San Francisco, CA.

Simmons, T. (1995, November 29). USF faculty back anti-bias policy. *Watermark*, p. 7.

Spradley, J. (1979). *The ethnographic interview*. New York: Holt, Reinhart & Winston.

Tierney, W. G., Bensimon, E. M., Frankel, C., Henderson, L., LaFlam, M., Locker, J., Marchesani, J., Rankin, S., Sumner, T., Upcraft, M. L., Walker, E. (1992). *Enhancing diversity: Toward a better campus climate. A report of the committee on lesbian and gay concerns*. University Park, PA: Pennsylvania State University.

Troiden, R. R. (1988). Homosexual identity development. *Journal of Adolescent Health Care*, 9 (2), pp. 105–113.

Urban, W. (1982). *Why teachers organize*. Detroit, MI: Wayne State University.

Uribe, V., & Harbeck, K. (1992). Addressing the needs of lesbian, gay, and bisexual youth: The origins of Project 10 and school-based intervention. In K. Harbeck (Ed.), *Coming out of the classroom closet: Gay and lesbian students, teachers, and curricula* (pp. 9–28). New York: Haworth.

Walling, D. (Ed.). (1996). *Open lives, safe schools*. Bloomington, IN: Phi Delta Kappa Educational Foundation.

The Weekly News. (1980, December 28). *Bush calls gays flea infested*. p. 1.

————. (1981, May 20). *The Bush amendment*, p. 12.

————. (1982, June 16). *Trask resigns*, p. 1, 8.

Weiss, A., & Schiller, G. (1988). *Before Stonewall: The making of a gay and lesbian community*. Tallahassee: Naiad.

Williams, W. (1991). Introduction. In J. Sears, *Growing up gay in the South: Race, gender, and journeys of the spirit*. New York: Haworth.

Wishik, H., & Pierce, C. (1995). *Sexual orientation and identity: Heterosexual, lesbian, gay, and bisexual journeys*. Lacuna, NH: New Dynamics Publications.

Woods, S., & Harbeck, K. (1992). Living in two worlds: The identity management strategies used by lesbian physical educators. In K. Harbeck (Ed.), *Coming out of the classroom closet: Gay and lesbian students, teachers, and curricula* (pp. 141–166). New York: Haworth.

Woog, D. (1995). *School's out: The impact of gay and lesbian issues on America's schools*. Boston: Alyson Publications, Inc.

Zuckerman, A., & Simons, G.(1994). *Sexual orientation in the workplace: Gay men, lesbians, bisexuals, & heterosexuals working together*. Santa Cruz, CA: International Partners Press.

Index

Abortion, 73, 99, 103

Abstinence, 103

Acanfora v. Board of Education of Montgomery County, 11

Acquired Immunodeficiency Virus (AIDS), 25, 29, 39, 45, 48, 49, 65, 66, 73, 74, 83, 99, 103, 110; *AIDS*, 73, 99.

Administrator, 43, 67, 75, 77, 81, 88, 93, 94, 97, 105, 117, 122, 125, 127; fear of, 94, 123; gay and lesbian, 70, 77, 90, 99, 128

Adoption, Florida law, 14–15, 18

Advocate, 29, 34, 100, 101, 121, 123, 125

American Federation of Teachers (AFT), 9, 12, 75, 88. *See also* Union

AIDS. *See* Acquired Immunodeficiency Virus

Allies, 29, 31, 92, 95, 98, 123, 126

Allied forces, World War II, 7

American Academy of Pediatrics, 9

American Counseling Association, 9

American Educational Researchers Association (AERA), 9

American Federation of Teachers (AFT), 9, 88

American Psychiatric Association (APA), 8, 9

American Psychological Association (APA), 8, 9

Anonymity, 23, 25–28, 34, 35, 114

Anti-discrimination, 17; legislation, 117

Anti-gay, 35, 48, 91, 95; adoption law, 14, 18; attitudes, 5, 17; bigotry, 15; harassment, 12, 125; resolution, 18. *See also* Adoption; Attitudes; Discrimination; Harassment

At-risk students, 97, 99, 100, 124, 126

Attitudes, 56, 57, 71, 72, 104; anti–gay, 17; homophobic, 13; school authorities, 11; societal, 10

Award. *See* Teacher of the Year

Baker County, 17, 23, 76

Baldwin, James, 102

Baptist. *See* First Baptist Church; Southern Baptist Convention

Baths. *See* City Bath Club

Berlin, 7
Bible, 6, 58, 73, 75, 99, 104, 108
Bisexual, 11, 13, 24, 74, 100
Black, 58, 59, 67; community, 116; students, 47, 63; triangle, 7. *See also* National Association for the Advancement of Colored People
Blume, Judy, 118
Blumenfeld, Warren, 131
Board of Education, 11, 12, 124, 125; Florida, 16, 17, 109; northeast Florida, 17. *See also* School board
Board of Regents, Florida. *See* Florida Board of Regents
Bo's Coral Reef, 87. *See also* Clubs
Boswell, John, 6
Boundary crossing, 32
Brevard County, 18
Brothers, 54, 71. *See also* Clubs
Broward County, 18, 109
Bryant, Anita, 14
Bush, Tom, 15–16
Bush-Trask Amendment, 15–16

California Supreme Court, 11
Canada, 24
Chamberlin, Don, 14–15
Christian Coalition, 17, 18, 83, 93, 104, 122; right wing groups, 23
Christian/un-Christian, 68, 104; principles, 104
Christianity, 6
Church, 23, 47, 65, 76, 83, 87, 104, 105, 122. *See also* Southern Baptist Convention
Circuit Court, 12
City Bath Club, 54, 91
Civil rights, 8; 1964 Civil Rights Act, 14. *See also* Equal, rights; Florida Civil Rights Act
Clay County, 17, 23, 76
Climate, 29, 34, 125, 126; cultural, 83; local, 104, 105; oppressive,

68; political, 23, 104; religious, 104; schools, 107–108
Clubs, 51, 53, 54, 63, 64, 87, 91, 96
Coach, 108
Coding the data, 29, 30
Colleagues, 5, 11, 12, 29, 33, 34, 81; distancing from, 112. *See also* Co-workers; Peers
College, 11, 36, 46, 48, 50, 53, 67, 69, 79, 112, 118, 128; community college, 118; courses, 117; professors, 13; students, 8, 132. *See also* University
Colorado Amendment Two, 11, 102
Come out (coming out), 5, 8–10, 12, 44, 47, 49, 52, 57, 60, 63, 67, 72, 75, 76, 84, 87–88, 98; at school, 100, 105
Communication, 91, 122; lack of, 90; system, 90
Communion, 54
Community, 2, 25, 29, 40, 55, 56, 70, 75, 85, 86, 123; Black, 116; culture, 81, 104; educational, 82, 106; intolerance, 9; lesbian, 24; lesbian and gay, 15, 18, 24–25, 31, 32, 33, 40, 55, 58, 60, 70, 82, 88–89, 105, 122, 128; military, 82; religious, 83; school, 125
Concentration camps, 7
Confidentiality, 24, 26
Conflict, 88, 111, 117
Conflicting viewpoints, 89
Conspiracy of silence, 115. *See also* Silence
Cop-out, 57
Counselors, 42, 45, 66, 101, 107, 117, 126, 127; drug, 110; gay, 71; guidance, 40, 65, 72, 73
Courts, 61; California Supreme Court, 11; Circuit Court, 12; Federal Appeals Court, 18; Florida Supreme Court, 16, 99;

U.S. Supreme Court, 10, 11, 12, 102
Co-workers, 107, 115
Crane, Ichabod, 1
Crenshaw, Ander, 91
Culture, 9, 11, 12, 22, 29, 33, 81, 82, 89, 102, 104–105; lesbian and gay, 124; local, 128; school, 126; youth, 59
Curriculum, 45, 99, 102, 117, 118, 124, 127; rainbow, 46

Dade County, 14, 18
Data analysis, 28, 30
Daughters of Bilitis, 7
Da Vinci, Leonardo, 102
Department of Education. *See* Florida Department of Education
Department of Public Health, 103
Derogatory statements, 56, 58, 63, 64, 110, 127
Design of the study, 21
Developmental task, 97
Dignity for All Students Act, 125
Discovery, 106, 113; fear of, 18, 81, 85, 90, 100, 101, 103, 114, 116, 123; identity, 24, 27, 35, 82. *See also* Identity; Fear
Discrimination, 7, 8, 10, 11, 14, 17, 18, 29, 33, 34, 44, 57, 76, 82, 94, 100, 101, 105, 109, 121–128; confronting, 111; freedom from, 124; in schools, 109, 110; job, 9; laws, 109; sanctioned, 129
Diversity, 9, 16, 100, 102
Domestic partner, 25, 35, 37–38, 39, 41, 43, 44, 47, 52, 53, 54, 57, 59, 60–62, 64, 65, 67, 68, 69, 71, 72, 74, 83, 128
Domestic partner benefits, 18, 104, 106, 112, 117
Drag queen, 39
Duberman, Martin, 6
Duval County, 17, 23,

Education, 9, 10, 13, 16, 40, 56, 66, 67, 99, 109, 125; field of, 1, 26, 33; higher education, 15, 16; majors, 46; policy, 109; process, 221; recertification, 117, 118; sexuality, 2; training, 8, 117, 118. *See also* Florida Department of Education
Educational leadership, 79, 125–126, 128
Empirical data, 22
Employment, 107, 109, 119, 125, 128, 129. *See also* Florida State Employment Policy
Employment Non-Discrimination Act (ENDA), 11
Episcopal Church, 76, 104
Equal: access, 12, 32; opportunity, 124, 132; protection, 11, 100; rights, 7, 14
Equity, 100
Ethical concerns, 27–28
Ethics, 28, 71, 72, 97; Florida Senate, 16. *See also* Florida Department of Education Code of Ethics

Faculty, 16, 44, 45, 52, 55, 64, 127; advisor, 101; lesbian and gay, 128; University of South Florida faculty senate, 16–17
Faculty senate, University of South Florida, 16–17
Faggot, 110
Falwell, Jerry, 17
Fear, 29, 35, 39, 67, 69, 74, 121, 123, 124, 128; internalized, 9; job loss, 30, 38, 81, 82, 83, 85, 90, 98, 100, 107, 114, 122, 124, 127; living in, 12, 13; modeling, 101; of colleagues, 108; of discovery, 18, 24, 85, 90, 100, 101, 103, 106, 113, 114 123. *See also* Filter of fear
Federal Appeals Court, 18
Federal Task Force, 97

Feminist, 70; perspectives, 5
Filter of fear, 81, 85, 90, 95, 100,
    101, 103, 108, 111, 114, 116
First Amendment, 10, 11, 16
First Baptist Church, 23, 47, 65, 76,
    104, 105
Florida Board of Regents, 16, 17
Florida Civil Rights Act, 17, 109,
    124
Florida Community College at
    Jacksonville, 128
Florida Department of Education,
    16, 29, 112
Florida Department of Education
    Code of Ethics, 40, 99, 105,
    109, 110, 125
Florida Department of Education
    Principles of Professional Prac-
    tice, 40, 99, 105, 109, 110, 125
Florida Hate Crimes Act, 109, 125
Florida International University, 16
Florida Legislative Investigative
    Committee, 13; Johns Com-
    mittee, 13
Florida Legislature, 13, 14, 18
Florida State Employment Policy,
    17, 109, 124
Florida State University System,
    16. *See also* Florida Board of
    Regents
Florida Supreme Court, 16, 99
Florida Task Force, 16
Ft. Lauderdale, 15
Fourteenth Amendment, 11
Fourteenth century, 6
Freedom, 77, 84; from discrimina-
    tion, 124, 125, 129
Freedom of speech, 10, 16
Friends, 37, 39, 46, 49, 52, 53, 54,
    57, 61, 63, 69, 87, 127; work
    related, 94
Friendship, 52; network, 34, 67
Frustration, 38, 42, 52, 98, 113,
    114, 124
Fundamentalist religious organiza-
    tions, 17–18, 81, 105. *See also*

First Baptist Church; Christian
    Coalition; Southern Baptist
    Convention

Gainesville, 18
Gay and lesbian pride, 18, 87, 106;
    Jacksonville, 64, 87
Gay Lesbian Straight Educators
    Network (GLSEN), 87, 109,
    126, 127, 131
Gay Liberation Front, 8
Gaylord v. Tacoma School District,
    11
Gay Straight Alliance (GSA), 31,
    126
Germany, 6–7; Penal Code 175, 7
Gittings, Barbara, 8
GLSEN. *See* Gay Lesbian Straight
    Educators Network
Graham, Bob, 16
Greenwich Village, 8
Griffin, Patricia, 5, 98

Harassment, 29, 33, 34, 40, 41, 50,
    61, 81, 87, 90, 107, 109, 111,
    115, 121, 123, 126, 127, 127;
    police, 8; policy, 40; prevention,
    112; sexual, 12, 55. *See also*
    Anti-gay
Harbeck, Karen, 8, 9, 12, 79, 97,
    100, 112–113, 131
Harlem Renaissance, 102
Harvard Law Review, 10–11
Hate, 55, 57, 59, 65, 67, 113. *See
    also* Florida Hate Crimes Act
Heterosexual (adj.) 2, 5, 8, 15, 24,
    42, 75, 85, 86, 96, 97, 115; al-
    lies, 31; colleagues, 123, 129;
    students, 121
Heterosexual (n.), 9; passing as,
    111–112
Hierarchy, educational, 128
High school, 48, 49, 50, 59, 60, 62,
    63, 68, 72, 85, 87, 91; Junior
    high school, 48
Hirschfeld, Magnus, 6

History, 102; of lesbian and gay
    people, 124; National Lesbian
    and Gay History Month, 127
Hitler, Adolph, 7
HIV. *See* Human Immunodefi-
    ciancy Virus
Homeless, 67
Homophobia, 87, 92, 97, 13, 24,
    126; internalized, 35, 89; insti-
    tutionalized, 38; pressures of,
    86
Homosexual (adj.), 8, 9, 10, 14, 16,
    33, 42, 49, 74, 121; orientation,
    84, 86, 90, 102, 107, 113. *See
    also* Identity
Homosexual (n.), 11, 14, 17, 24, 25
Homosexuality, 66, 73, 99
*Homosexuality and Citizenship in
    Florida*, 13
Hooker, Evelyn, 8
Human Immunodeficiancy Virus
    (HIV) 25, 29, 45, 48, 65, 83.
    See also Acquired Immunodefi-
    ciency Virus

Identity, 24, 27, 30, 83; discovery,
    82; homosexual, 33; lesbian and
    gay, 26; management, 111, 113,
    128; sexual, 5, 10, 45, 48, 84,
    111; sexual identity develop-
    ment, 128
Inquiry, 26, 56, 121
In-service, 46, 117, 118
Institute of Sexual Science, 7
Interpretation, 29, 30, 31; of data,
    79, 82, 121
Interpretive model, 79, 81, 82, 85,
    86, 88, 90, 91, 93–96, 100, 101,
    103, 105, 106, 108, 111, 114,
    116, 119; triangle, 82
Interview, 21–23, 25, 26, 28, 30–
    34, 41, 42, 43, 48, 60, 62, 68,
    79, 82–85, 104, 106
In Touch, 73. *See also* Clubs
Invisibility, 9, 12, 11, 114, 122

Isolation, 79, 81, 82, 86, 88, 90, 91,
    93, 97, 98, 101, 106, 108, 121,
    128; field of, 88–91; from peers,
    2

Jacksonville Area Sexual Minority
    Youth Network (JASMYN), 45,
    65, 73, 87, 122
Jacksonville, City of, 17, 18, 48,
    54, 64, 65, 70, 73, 87, 91, 106,
    109; Chamber of Commerce, 23
Jacksonville Gay and Lesbian
    Pride, 64; committee, 87
Jacksonville University, 128
James I, 58, 102
JASMYN. *See* Jacksonville Area
    Sexual Minority Youth Net-
    work
Job satisfaction, 29
Johns, Charley, 13
Johns Committee, 13; Florida
    Legislative Investigative Com-
    mittee, 13
Johns report, *Homosexuality and
    Citizenship in Florida*, 13
Junior high school, 48

Katz, Jonathan, 6, 9
Key West, 18, 109
Khayatt, Madyha, 24, 27, 32
King James. *See* James I
Kissen, Rita, 26, 85, 86, 88, 90, 92,
    94, 101, 112, 115, 131

Label, 29; computer, 30
Language, 22, 33, 40, 103, 127;
    discriminatory, 127; policy, 17;
    prejudicial, 39, 107, 110
Leadership. *See* Educational lead-
    ership
Legal cases: *Acanfora v. Board of
    Education of Montgomery
    County,* 11; *Gaylord v. Tacoma
    School District,* 11; *Morrison v.
    California Board of Education,*
    11; *Nabozny v. Podlesny,* 12,

131; *Roland v. Mad River School District*, 10–11

Legal, action, 129; initiatives, 124; protection, 11, 12, 17; review, 5; support, 12

Lesbian and Gay Community Association of Jacksonville (LGCAJ), 87

Legislature, Florida, 13, 14, 18

Litigation, 12

Little Dude, 70. *See also* Clubs

Loss, 116; financial, 9; job, 30, 81, 82, 84, 85, 90, 92, 98, 100, 101, 103, 107, 122–124; of partner, 35, 92

Lying, 38, 50, 61, 66, 116; to colleagues, 5; to students, 5

March on Washington, 38

Marginalization, 122

Marriage, 57, 103; same sex, 18

Masturbation, 66, 73, 99

Mattachine Society, 7

Mayport Mary, 69

McCarthyism, 7

Mead, Margaret, 58, 102

Media, 8, 23, 81, 82; lesbian and gay, 24

Methodology, 21

Metropolitan Community Church, 87

Miami, 16, 109

Miami Beach, 18

Military, 75, 82

Model, of morality, 31. *See also* Role model

Molestation, 35

Monitor, by citizens, 2

Moral Majority, 17; Falwell, Jerry, 17

Moral standards, 2, 16, 18

Moral turpitude, 71, 111, 112

Morgan, Ellen, 18

Morrison v. California Board of Education, 11

Multicultural, 75, 105; education, 118

Myth, 24

Nabozny, Jamie, 12

Nabozny v. Podlesny, 12, 131

Nassau County, 17, 23

National Association for the Advancement of Colored People (NAACP), 13

National Association of Social Workers, 9

National Consortium of Directors of Lesbian, Gay, Bisexual, and Transgender Resources in Higher Education, 131

National Council of Accreditation on Teacher Education (NCATE), 9

National Education Association (NEA), 9, 12, 18–19, 132

National Lesbian and Gay History Month, 127

Nazis, 7

Nigger, 58, 59, 75

Nineteenth Amendment, 14

Non-discrimination, 16, 17, 18; policy, 109

Northeast Florida, 21–26, 29, 31–34, 79, 82–85, 87–93, 99, 100, 104–106, 109, 111, 113, 115, 118, 121–124, 126–129

Nurse, 39

Ombudsperson, 125

Oppression, 92, 107, 114, 115, 126; paradox of, 92

Orlando, 18

Pagoda, 70

Palm Beach, 109

Parents, 29, 34, 42, 49, 50, 98, 123, 126, 127; of students, 45, 55, 65, 66, 67, 73, 74, 94–95, 103, 107, 115, 118, 119

Parents and Friends of Lesbians and Gays (PFLAG), 87, 127, 131
Participatory consciousness, 28
Partner. *See* Domestic partner
Paxson Communications, 18
Peers, 116; of students, 47, 105. *See also* Colleagues
PFLAG. *See* Parents and Friends of Lesbians and Gays
Phil Donahue Show, 15
Plato, 102
Porter, Cole, 102
Power, 7, 9,14, 32, 73, 79, 81, 82, 90, 95, 105, 108, 116, 119, 123
Prevention programs, 126
Pride. *See* Gay and lesbian pride; Jacksonville Gay and Lesbian Pride
Principal, 37, 39, 40, 45, 47, 52, 55, 61, 64, 69, 70, 73, 74, 81, 83, 90, 93, 95, 101, 108, 110, 113, 115
Principles of Professional Practice. *See* Florida Department of Education Principles of Professional Practice
Public health, Department, 103

Queer, 40, 49, 74, 76, 81, 105, 107, 110, 111

Rainbow, curriculum, 46
Recertification, 46, 117, 118, 128
Regents, Florida Board of , 16, 17
Relationship, 25, 29, 38, 49, 51, 53, 60, 62, 68, 95, 98, 112, 113; with colleagues, 56, 98, 115; with students, 95, 97
Religion, 29; role of, 2
Reparative therapy, 9
Research questions, 21, 22, 34
Rich, Adrienne, 114
Robertson, Pat, 18
Roland v. Mad River School District. *See* Legal Cases

Role model, 12, 34, 58, 60, 65, 67, 76, 77, 83, 84, 97–100, 102, 103, 114, 121, 123, 126; theory, 11

Safe, 10, 12, 18, 22, 29, 33, 45, 58, 72, 73, 90, 94, 111, 124, 127, 128, 129; schools, 92, 104, 108; environment, 31, 88, 117, 127, 128, 129; personal safety, 90, 111; psychological safety, 124; safety, 123, 124; unsafe, 121
St. Augustine, 6, 70
St. Johns County, 17, 23, 76
Scientific Humanitarian Committee, 6
School board, 61, 65, 70, 76, 81, 87, 93, 95, 103, 104. *See also* Board of Education
Sears, James, 9, 12, 13, 14, 23, 24, 121, 132
Secrecy, 18; secret, 84, 85, 98
Self, 28, 29; discovery, 32; protection, 115; self–select, 26, 79; separateness of, 89, 90
Seminary, 36, 48
Senate, Florida, 14, 16; United States, 11; University of South Florida, 16–17
Sensitive research, 27
Sexuality, human, 27
Sexual orientation, 21, 24, 25, 28, 31, 32, 34, 40, 45, 46, 57, 65, 73, 84–86, 90, 92–94, 97, 98, 103, 107, 109, 111, 114, 115, 117; and education, 5, 8; and invisibility, 11; discrimination, 11, 12; harassment, 6, 12; inclusion, 12; of teachers, 3; policies, 9, 16, 17, 18, 124, 125; revealing, 9, 12, 16; young people, 97, 101, 107
Sexuality, 40, 65, 69, 87, 100
Shame, 84, 98, 115
Shepard, Matthew, 17
Signorile, Michelangelo, 84

Silence, 6, 8, 13, 19, 21, 35, 90 92,
    94, 114–116, 121–124; conspir-
    acy of, 115; silent, 97, 114–115,
    119, 129
Social support, 93, 122
South, 12, 14, 15, 23, 24, 38, 75,
    104, 132
Southern Baptist Convention, 18,
    23, 83, 122
Southerners, 23
Speech, freedom of, 10, 16
Spring of Life homes, 7
Staff, 64, 67, 88, 101, 127, 128
Standard, 50, 112
Stein, Gertrude, 102
Stereotype, 44, 76
Stonewall, 8
Stress, 86, 92, 93, 106, 122, 123
Students, 23, 38, 45, 52, 53, 62, 63,
    67, 71, 72, 73, 76, 81, 83–85,
    87, 89, 91, 92, 93, 95–119, 121,
    123–125, 129; college, 8; har-
    assment of, 12; lesbian and gay,
    27, 29, 34, 41, 42, 45, 51, 62,
    63, 71, 72, 76, 83, 91, 104, 108,
    114, 126–128
Suicide, 72, 97; Federal Task Force
    report; prevention, 126
Superintendent, 69, 76, 104, 112

Taboos, 114
Teacher of the Year Award, 25, 89
Tension, 41
Tenure, 67
Terminology, 81, 105
Theoretical screen, 30–31, 79
Theoretical framework, 31
Theory, 31
The Weekly News, 15, 16, 17
Tilden, Bill, 102
Tolerance, 23, 24, 104
Transgender, 24
Trask, 15, 16; Bush-Trask
    Amendment, 15–16

Triangle, black, 7; pink, 7, red, 7;
    in interpretive model, 82
Tschaikowsky, Peter, 102
Turing, Alan, 102
Turpitude. See Moral turpitude
Twilight world, 7

Ulrichs, Karl, 6
Un-Christian. See Christian/un-
    Christian
Union, 41, 61, 69, 71. See also
    American Federation of Teach-
    ers; National Education Asso-
    ciation
United States, (n.), 5, 6, 7, 8, 13;
    teachers in, 2
U.S. House UnAmerican Activities
    Committee, 7
United States Supreme Court, 10,
    11, 12, 102
University, 8, 15, 16, 17, 128. See
    also College
University of South Florida (USF),
    faculty senate, 16–17
University of North Florida (UNF),
    74, 87, 109, 118, 128

Values, 16, 22, 30, 31, 32; conser-
    vative, 23; of homophobia, 89;
    of locale, 2
Violence, 105
Vulnerable, 58, 68, 113, 114, 115,
    124

Walt Disney Corporation, 18
Whitman, Walt, 102
Wilson, Lori, 14–15
Wisconsin, University of, 12
WJXT Channel Four, 99
World League for Sexual Reform,
    7

World Wide Web, 99

About the Author

RONNI L. SANLO is Director of the Lesbian, Gay, Bisexual and Transgender Resources Center at UCLA.

ISBN 0-89789-640-8

HARDCOVER BAR CODE